Elisha Kent Kane

The Far North

Exploration in the Arctic regions

Elisha Kent Kane

The Far North
Exploration in the Arctic regions

ISBN/EAN: 9783337325305

Printed in Europe, USA, Canada, Australia, Japan

Cover: Foto ©Andreas Hilbeck / pixelio.de

More available books at **www.hansebooks.com**

EXPLORATIONS IN

THE ARCTIC REGIONS.

BY

ELISHA KENT KANE, M.D.,

COMMANDER, SECOND "GRINNELL" EXPEDITION IN SEARCH OF
SIR JOHN FRANKLIN.

PREFACE.

In May 1845, Sir John Franklin sailed from England with the ships *Erebus* and *Terror*, on an expedition to attempt the discovery of a "North-West Passage," or water communication between the Atlantic and Pacific Oceans, to the North of the American Continent. No intelligence was received from him after the year following.

Numerous expeditions were fitted out and despatched in search of Franklin and his brave crew, both from this country and from America. In 1854, Dr Rae returned with information that the Esquimaux had reported having seen the bodies of "forty white men," near Great Fish River, in the spring of 1850. This intelligence was not considered trustworthy, and Lady Franklin fitted out a private expedition, under the command of Captain M'Clintock, who sailed from Aberdeen in the steam-yacht *Fox*, July 1857. He returned in 1859 with indisputable proofs of the death of Franklin, and the fate of the expedition under his command,—full details of which he afterwards published.*

The present volume is an epitome of "Arctic Explorations," † an official account of the Second "Grinnell" Expedition in search of Sir John Franklin,—the First Grinnell Expedition having been despatched in 1850 under Lieutenant De Haven, with Dr Kane as surgeon. These expeditions were fitted out at New York, at the expense of a wealthy and generous merchant of that city, named Grinnell, and Mr Peabody, the eminent American resident in London, whose munificence and liberality are now so well known in this country. In the Second Expedition, the brig *Advance* was placed under the command of Dr Elisha Kent Kane, assistant-surgeon, U.S.N., a gentleman well qualified, from previous experience, to undertake such an important duty.

Dr Kane was born at Philadelphia in 1822, and was educated at the Medical College of Pennsylvania. In 1843 he accompanied the U.S. embassy to China, and for some time travelled in the interior of India. He also explored the Nile as far as the frontiers of Nubia. Returning to America, he afterwards visited the slave-coasts of Africa. He served in the U.S. army for a short period, and underwent many hardships during the Mexican campaign. In 1853 he was appointed to the command of the Arctic Expedition, a detailed narrative of which is contained in the present volume. Dr Kane died at Havannah in 1857, at the early age of thirty-five.

* A Narrative of the Discovery of the Fate of Sir John Franklin and his Companions. By Captain F. L. M'Clintock, R.N., LL.D. 8vo 1859.

† Arctic Explorations: the Second Grinnell Expedition in Search of Sir John Franklin, 1853-55. By Elisha Kent Kane, M.D., U.S.N. 2 vols 8vo. 1856.

CONTENTS.

		PAGE
CHAP. I.	Organisation—New York to the North Water,	9
CHAP. II.	The North Water to the Wintering Ground,	18
CHAP. III.	Our First Walk Out—The Depôt Party,	34
CHAP. IV.	Domestic Troubles—Return of the Depôt Party,	43
CHAP. V.	Our First Winter,	50
CHAP. VI.	An Anxious Search,	60
CHAP. VII.	The First Strange Faces—The Esquimaux,	74
CHAP. VIII.	A new Exploration—Return of Spring,	83
CHAP. IX.	Advent of the Second Year,	93
CHAP. X.	The North-East Party,	100
CHAP. XI.	Attempt to Reach Beechy Island,	113
CHAP. XII.	The Second Winter—Departure of half of the Crew,	124
CHAP. XIII.	Negotiations with the Esquimaux,	133
CHAP. XIV.	The Esquimaux Village—A Walrus Hunt,	150
CHAP. XV.	The Coming Winter,	157
CHAP. XVI.	Preparation for Leaving the Brig,	168
CHAP. XVII.	Farewell to the "Advance,"	181
CHAP. XVIII.	The March and its Incidents,	191
CHAP. XIX.	Our March over Land and Sea,	205
CHAP. XX.	Starvation—Plenty—The Escape Welcome,	222
CHAP. XXI.	Conclusion,	227

THE FAR NORTH.

CHAPTER I.

ORGANIZATION—NEW YORK TO THE NORTH WATER.

In the month of December 1852, I had the honour of receiving special orders from the Secretary of the Navy of the United States, to "conduct an expedition to the Arctic Seas in search of Sir John Franklin."

I had been engaged, under Lieutenant De Haven, in the Grinnell Expedition, which sailed from the United States in 1850 on the same errand; and I had occupied myself for some months after our return in maturing the scheme of a renewed effort to rescue the missing party, or at least to resolve the mystery of its fate. Mr Grinnell, with a liberality altogether characteristic, had placed the *Advance*, in which I sailed before, at my disposal for the cruise; and Mr Peabody of London, the generous representative of many American sympathies, had proffered his aid largely toward her outfit. The Geographical Society of New York, the Smithsonian Institution, the American Philosophical Society, and a number of scientific associations aid friends of science besides, had come forward to help me; and by their aid I managed to secure a better outfit for purposes of observation than would otherwise have been possible to a party so limited in numbers, and absorbed in other objects.

Ten of our little party belonged to the United States Navy, and were attached to my command by orders from the Department; the others were shipped by me for the cruise, and at salaries entirely disproportioned to their services: all were volunteers. We did not sail under the rules that govern our national ships; but we had our own regulations, well considered and announced beforehand, and rigidly adhered to afterward through all the vicissitudes of the expedition. These included—first, absolute subordination to the officer in command, or his delegate; second, abstinence from all intoxicating liquors, except when dispensed by special order; third, the habitual disuse of profane language. We had no other laws.

All hands counted, we were eighteen at the time of sailing. Another joined us a few days afterward; so that the party under my command, as it reached the coast of Greenland, consisted of—

ELISHA KENT KANE, Commander.

HENRY BROOKS, First Officer.	ISAAC I. HAYES, M.D., Surgeon.
JOHN WALL WILSON.	AUGUST SONTAG, Astronomer.
JAMES M'GARY.	AMOS BONSALL.
GEORGE RILEY.	GEORGE STEPHENSON.
WILLIAM MORTON.	GEORGE WHIPPLE.
CHRISTIAN OHLSEN.	WILLIAM GODFREY.
HENRY GOODFELLOW.	JOHN BLAKE.

JEFFERSON BAKER.
PETER SCHUBERT.
THOMAS HICKEY.

Two of these, Brooks and Morton, had been my associates

in the first expedition; gallant and trustworthy men, both of them, as ever shared the fortunes or claimed the gratitude of a commander.

The *Advance* had been thoroughly tried in many encounters with the Arctic ice. She was carefully inspected, and needed very little to make her all a seaman could wish. She was a brig of one hundred and forty-four tons, intended originally for carrying heavy castings from an iron-foundry, but strengthened afterward with great skill and at large expense. She was a good sailor, and easily managed. We had five boats; one of them a metallic life-boat.

Our equipment consisted of little else than a quantity of rough boards, to serve for housing over the vessel in winter, some tents of India-rubber and canvas, of the simplest description, and several carefully-built sledges, some of them on a model furnished me by the kindness of the British Admiralty, others of my own devising.

Our store of provisions was chosen with little regard to luxury. We took with us some two thousand pounds of well-made pemmican,* a parcel of Borden's meat-biscuit, some packages of an exsiccated potato, resembling Edwards's, some pickled cabbage, and a liberal quantity of American dried fruits and vegetables; besides these, we had the salt beef and pork of the navy ration, hard biscuit, and flour. A very moderate supply of liquors, with the ordinary *et ceteras* of an Arctic cruiser, made up the diet-list. I hoped to procure some fresh provisions in addition, before reaching the upper coast of Greenland; and I carried some barrels of malt, with a compact apparatus for brewing.

We had a moderate wardrobe of woollens, a full supply

---

* *Pemmican*, cured meat, pulverized, mixed with fat and packed in hermetically sealed cases.

of knives, needles, and other articles for barter, a large, well-chosen library, and a valuable set of instruments for scientific observations.

We left New York on the 30th of May 1853, escorted by several noble steamers; and, passing slowly on to the Narrows amid salutes and cheers of farewell, cast our brig off from the steam-tug and put to sea.

It took us eighteen days to reach St John's, Newfoundland. The Governor, Mr Hamilton, a brother of the Secretary of the Admiralty, received us with a hearty English welcome; and all the officials, indeed all the inhabitants, vied with each other in efforts to advance our views. I purchased here a stock of fresh beef, which, after removing the bones and tendons, we compressed into rolls by wrapping it closely with twine, according to the nautical process of *marling*, and hung it up in the rigging.

After two days we left this thriving and hospitable city; and, with a noble team of Newfoundland dogs on board, the gift of Governor Hamilton, headed our brig for the coast of Greenland.

We reached Baffin's Bay without incident. We took deep-sea-soundings as we approached its axis, and found a reliable depth of nineteen hundred fathoms: an interesting result, as it shows that the ridge, which is known to extend between Ireland and Newfoundland in the bed of the Atlantic, is depressed as it passes further to the north. A few days more found us off the coast of Greenland, making our way toward Fiskernaes, the harbour of which we entered on the 1st of July, amid the clamour of its entire population, assembled on the rocks to greet us.

We found Mr Lassen, the superintending official of the Danish Company, a hearty single-minded man, fond of his wife, his children, and his pipe. The visit of our brig was, of course, an incident to be marked in the simple annals of his colony; and, even before I had shown him my official letter from the Court of Denmark, he had most hospitably proffered everything for our accommodation. We became his guests, and interchanged presents with him before our departure; this last transaction enabling me to say, with confidence, that the inner fiords* produce noble salmon-trout; and that the reindeer-tongue, a recognised delicacy in the old and new Arctic continents, is justly appreciated at Fiskernaes.

Feeling that our dogs would require fresh provisions, which could hardly be spared from our supplies on shipboard, I availed myself of Mr Lassen's influence to obtain an Esquimaux hunter for our party. He recommended to me one Hans Christian, a boy of nineteen, as an expert with the kayak and javelin; and after Hans had given me a touch of his quality by spearing a bird on the wing, I engaged him. He was fat, good-natured, and, except under the excitements of the hunt, very stolid and unimpressible. He stipulated that, in addition to his very moderate wages, I should leave a couple of barrels of bread and fifty-two pounds of pork with his mother; and I became munificent in his eyes when I added the gift of a rifle and a new kayak. We found him very useful; our dogs required his services as a caterer, and our own table was more than once dependent on his energies.

Bidding good-bye to the governor, whose hospitality we had shared liberally, we put to sea on Saturday, the 10th, beating to the northward and westward in the teeth of a heavy gale.

From the time we left Fiskernaes, we had the usual delays from fogs and adverse currents, and did not reach

* *Fiord,* an abrupt inlet of the sea.

the neighbourhood of Wilcox Point, which defines Melville Bay, until the 27th of July.

On the 16th we passed the promontory of Swarte-huk, and were welcomed the next day at Proven by my old friend Christiansen, the superintendent, and found his family much as I left them three years before. Frederick, his son, had married a native woman, and added a summer tent, a half-breed boy, and a Danish rifle, to his stock of valuables. My former patient, Anna, had united fortunes with a fat-faced Esquimaux, and was the mother of a chubby little girl. Madame Christiansen, who counted all these and so many others as her happy progeny, was hearty and warm-hearted as ever. She led the household in sewing up my skins into various serviceable garments; and I had the satisfaction, before I left, of completing my stock of furs for our sledge parties.

Coasting along, we passed in succession the Esquimaux settlement of Kingatok, the Kettle—a mountain-top, so named from the resemblances of its profile—and finally Yotlik, the furthest point of colonisation; beyond which, save the sparse headlands of the charts, the coast may be regarded as unknown. Then, inclining more directly toward the north, we ran close to the Baffin Islands, sighted the landmark which is known as the Horse's Head, and passing the Duck Islands, bore away for Wilcox Point.

We stood lazily along the coast, with alternations of perfect calm and off-shore breezes, generally from the south or east; but on the morning of the 27th of July, as we neared the entrance of Melville Bay, a heavy ice-fog settled around us. We could hardly see across the decks, and yet were sensible of the action of currents carrying us we knew not where. By the time the sun had scattered the mist, Wilcox Point was to the south of us; and our little brig, now fairly in the bay, stood a fair chance of drifting over toward Devil's Thumb, which then bore east of north. The bergs which infest this region, and which have earned for it among the whalers the title of the " Bergy Hole," showed themselves all around us—we had come in among them in the fog.

It was a whole day's work, towing with both boats; but toward evening we had succeeded in crawling off shore, and were doubly rewarded for our labour with a wind. I had observed with surprise, while we were floating near the coast, that the land-ice was already broken and decayed; and I was aware, from what I had read, as well as what I had learned from whalers and observed myself of the peculiarities of this navigation, that the inshore track was in consequence beset with difficulty and delays. I made up my mind at once. I would stand to the westward until arrested by the pack,* and endeavour to *double* Melville Bay by an outside passage. A chronicle of this transit, condensed from my log-book, will interest the reader :—

"*July* 28.—Bore up to the northward and eastward, heading for Cape York in tolerably free water.

"*July* 29.—Entered broken ice, intending to work to the northward and eastward, above or about Sabine Islands, in search of the north-eastern land-ice. The breeze freshened off-shore, breaking up and sending out the floes, the leads† rapidly closing. Fearing a besetment, I determined to fasten to an iceberg; and after eight hours of very heavy labour, warping, heaving, and planting ice-anchors, succeeded in effecting it.

"We had hardly a breathing spell, before we were

* *Pack*, a large area of broken floating ice.
† *Lead*, a navigable opening in the ice.

startled by a set of loud, crackling sounds above us; and small fragments of ice, not larger than a walnut, began to dot the water like the first drops of a summer shower. The indications were too plain; we had barely time to cast off, before the face of the berg fell in ruins, crashing like artillery.

"Our position, in the mean time, had been critical, a gale blowing off the shore, and the floes closing and scudding rapidly. We lost some three hundred and sixty fathoms of whale-line, which were caught in the floes, and had to be cut away to release us from the drift. It was a hard night for boat-work, particularly with those of the party who were taking their first lessons in floe navigation.

"*July* 30.—Again moored alongside of an iceberg. Holding on for clearer weather. Two lively bears seen about 2 A.M. The 'Red Boat,' with Petersen and Hayes, got one; I took one of the quarter-boats, and shot the other.

"*August* 1.—Beset thoroughly with drifting ice, small rotten floe-pieces. But for our berg, we would now be carried to the south; as it is, we drift with it to the north and east.

"About 10 P.M. the immediate danger was past; and, espying a lead to the north-east, we got under weigh, and pushed over in spite of the drifting trash. The men worked with a will, and we bored through the floes in excellent style."

On our road we were favoured with a gorgeous spectacle, which hardly any excitement of peril could have made us overlook. The midnight sun came out over the northern crest of the great berg, our late "fast friend," kindling variously-coloured fires on every part of its surface, and

* *Floe*, a portion of ice detached from the main body.

making the ice around us one great resplendency of gem work, blazing carbuncles, and rubies and molten gold.

Our brig went crunching through all this jewellery; and, after a tortuous progress of five miles, arrested here and there by tongues which required the saw and ice-chisels, fitted herself neatly between two floes. Here she rested till toward morning, when the leads opened again, and I was able, from the crow's-nest, to pick our way to a larger pool some distance ahead. In this we beat backward and forward, like gold-fish seeking an outlet from a glass jar, till the fog caught us again; and so the day ended.

Everything now depended upon practical ice knowledge; and, as I was not willing to trust any one else in selecting the leads for our course, I spent the whole day with M'Gary at the mast-head.

At midnight we were clear of the bay and its myriads of discouragements. The North Water, our highway to Smith's Sound, was fairly ahead.

We succeeded, not without some laborious boring and serious risks of entanglement among the broken icefields. But we managed, in every instance, to combat this last form of difficulty by attaching our vessel to large icebergs, which enabled us to hold our own, however swiftly the surface floes were pressing by us to the south. Four days of this scarcely varied yet exciting navigation brought us to the extended fields of the pack, and a fortunate northwester opened a passage for us through them. We were now in the North Water.

CHAPTER II.

THE NORTH WATER TO THE WINTERING GROUND.

My diary continues:—"We passed the 'Crimson Cliffs' of Sir John Ross in the forenoon of August 5th. The patches of red snow, from which they derive their name, could be seen clearly at the distance of ten miles from the coast. It had a fine deep rose hue, and all the gorges and ravines in which the snows had lodged were deeply tinted with it. I had no difficulty now in justifying the somewhat poetical nomenclature which Sir John Franklin applied to this locality; for if the snowy surface were more diffused, as it is no doubt, earlier in the season, crimson would be the prevailing colour.

"Late at night we passed Conical Rock, the most insulated and conspicuous landmark of this coast; and, still later, Wolstenholme and Saunder's Islands, and Oomenak, the place of the *North Star's* winter-quarters—an admirable day's run; and so ends the 5th of August. We are standing along, with studding-sails set, and open water before us, fast nearing our scene of labour. We have already got to work, sewing up blanket bags and preparing sledges for our campaignings on the ice."

We reached Hakluyt Island in the course of the next day.

"*August* 6.—Cape Alexander and Cape Isabella, the headlands of Smith's Sound, are now in sight; and, in addition to these indications of our progress toward the field of search, a marked swell has set in after a short blow from the northward, just such as might be looked for from the action of the wind upon an open water-space beyond.

"*August* 7.—We have left Cape Alexander to the south; and Littleton Island is before us, hiding Cape Hatherton, the latest positively-determined headland. We are fairly inside of Smith's Sound.

"As we neared the west end of Littleton Island, after breakfast this morning, I ascended to the crow's-nest, and saw to my sorrow the ominous blink of ice ahead. The wind has been freshening for a couple of days from the northward, and if it continues, it will bring down the floes on us.

"My mind has been made up from the first that we are to force our way to the north, as far as the elements will let us; and I feel the importance, therefore, of securing a place of retreat, that in case of disaster we may not be altogether at large. Besides, we have now reached one of the points at which, if any one is to follow us, he might look for some trace to guide him."

I determined to leave a cairn on Littleton Island, and to deposit a boat with a supply of stores in some convenient place near it. One of our whale-boats had been crushed in Melville Bay, and the metallic life-boat was the only one I could spare. Its length did not exceed twenty feet, and our crew of twenty could hardly stow themselves in it, with even a few days' rations; but it was air-chambered and buoyant.

Selecting from our stock of provisions and field equipage such portions as we might by good luck be able to dispense with, and adding with reluctant liberality some blankets and a few yards of India-rubber cloth, we set out in search of a spot for our first depôt. It was essential that it should be upon the mainland, for the rapid tides might so wear away the ice as to make an island inaccessible to a foot-party; and yet it was desirable that, while secure against the action of sea and ice, it should be approachable by boats. We found such a place after some pretty cold rowing. It was off the north-east cape of Littleton, and bore S.S.E. from Cape Hatherton, which loomed in the distance above the fog. Here were buried our life-boat with her little cargo. We placed along her gunwale the heaviest rocks we could handle, and, filling up the interstices with smaller stones and sods of andromeda and moss, poured sand and water among the layers. This, frozen at once into a solid mass, might be hard enough, we hoped, to resist the claws of the polar bear.

We found to our surprise that we were not the first human beings who had sought a shelter in this desolate spot. A few ruined walls here and there showed that it had once been the seat of a rude settlement; and in the little knoll which we cleared away to cover in our storehouse of valuables, we found the mortal remains of their former inhabitants.

Nothing can be imagined more sad and homeless than these memorials of extinct life. Hardly a vestige of growth was traceable on the bare ice-rubbed rocks; and the huts resembled so much the broken fragments that surrounded them, that at first sight it was hard to distinguish one from the other. Walrus-bones lay about in all directions, showing that this animal had furnished the staple of subsistence. There were some remains, too, of the fox and the narwhal;* but I found no signs of the seal or reindeer.

These Esquimaux have no mother earth to receive their dead, but seat them as in the attitude of repose, the knees

* *Narwhal*, the sea unicorn.

drawn close to the body, and enclose them in a sack of skins. The implements used by the person while living are then grouped around him; they are covered with a rude dome of stones, and a cairn is piled above. This simple cenotaph will remain intact for generation after generation. The Esquimaux never disturb a grave.

Our stores deposited, it was our next office to erect a beacon, and intrust to it our tidings. We chose for this purpose the Western Cape of Littleton Island, as more conspicuous than Cape Hatherton; built our cairn; wedged a staff into the crevices of the rocks; and, spreading the American flag, hailed its folds with three cheers as they expanded in the cold midnight breeze. These important duties performed—the more lightly, let me say, for this little flicker of enthusiasm—we rejoined the brig early on the morning of the 7th, and forced on again towards the north, beating against wind and tide.

"*August* 8.—I had seen the ominous blink ahead of us from the Flagstaff Point of Littleton Island, and before two hours were over, we closed with ice to the westward.

"In the evening I ventured out again with the change of tide, but it was only to renew a profitless conflict. The flood, encountering the southward movement of the floes, drove them in upon the shore, and with such rapidity and force as to carry the smaller bergs along with them. We were too happy, when, after a manful struggle of some hours, we found ourselves once more out of their range.

"Our new position was rather nearer to the south than the one we had left. It was in a beautiful cove, land-locked from east to west, and accessible only from the north. Here we moored our vessel securely by hawsers to the rocks and a whale-line carried out to the narrow entrance. At M'Gary's suggestion, I called it 'Fog

Inlet;' but we afterwards remembered it more thankfully as REFUGE HARBOUR.

"*August* 9.—It may be noted among our little miseries, that we have more than fifty dogs on board, the majority of which might rather be characterised as 'ravening wolves.' To feed this family, upon whose strength our progress and success depend, is really a difficult matter. The absence of shore or land ice to the south in Baffin's Bay has prevented our rifles from contributing any material aid to our commissariat. Our two bears lasted the cormorants but eight days; and to feed them upon the meagre allowance of two pounds of raw flesh every other day, is an almost impossible necessity. Only yesterday they were ready to eat the caboose up, for I would not give them pemmican. Corn-meal or beans they disdain to touch, and salt junk would kill them.

"Accordingly I started out this morning to hunt walrus, with which the Sound is teeming. We saw at least fifty of these dusky monsters, and approached many groups within twenty paces; but our rifle balls reverberated from their hides like cork pellets from a pop-gun target, and we could not get within harpoon-distance of one. Later in the day, however, Ohlsen, climbing a neighbouring hill to scan the horizon, and see if the ice had slackened, found the dead carcase of a narwhal—a happy discovery, which has secured for us at least six hundred pounds of good wholesome flesh. The length of the narwhal was fourteen feet, and his process, or 'horn,' from the tip to its bony encasement, four feet. We built a fire on the rocks, and melted down his blubber; he will yield readily two barrels of oil."

With the small hours of Wednesday morning came a breeze from the south-west, which was followed by such an apparent relaxation of the floes at the slack-water of flood tide, that I resolved to attempt an escape from our little basin.

"*August* 12.—After careful consideration, I have determined to try for a further northing, by following the coastline. At certain stages of the tides—generally from three-quarters flood to the commencement of the ebb—the ice evidently relaxes enough to give a partial opening close along the land. The strength of our vessel we have tested pretty thoroughly; if she will bear the frequent groundings that we must look for, I am persuaded we may seek these openings, and warp along them from one lump of grounded ice to another. The water is too shallow for ice-masses to float in, that are heavy enough to make a nip very dangerous. I am preparing the little brig for this novel navigation, clearing her decks, securing things below with extra lashings, and getting out spars, to serve in case of necessity as shores to keep her on an even keel.

"*August* 14.—Change of weather yesterday tempted us to forsake our shelter and try another tussle with the ice. We met it as soon as we ventured out; and the day closed with a northerly progress, by hard warping, of about three-quarters of a mile. The men were well tired, but the weather looked so threatening, that I had them up again at three o'clock this morning. My immediate aim is to attain a low rocky island which we see close into the shore, about a mile ahead of us.

"*Midnight.*—We did reach it, and just in time. At 11.30 P.M., our first whale-line was made fast to the rocks. Ten minutes later, the breeze freshened, and so directly in our teeth that we could not have gained our mooring-ground. It is blowing a gale now, and the ice driving to the northward before it; but we can rely upon our hawsers. All behind us is now solid pack.

"*August* 16.—Fast still; the wind dying out, and the ice outside closing steadily. And here, for all I can see, we must hang on for the winter, unless Providence shall send a smart ice-shattering breeze to open a road for us to the northward.

"More bother with these wretched dogs! worse than a street of Constantinople emptied upon our decks; the unruly, thieving, wild-beast pack! Not a bear's paw, nor an Esquimaux cranium, or basket of mosses, or any specimen whatever, can leave your hands for a moment, without their making a rush at it, and, after a yelping scramble, swallowing it at a gulp. I have seen them attempt a whole feather-bed; and here, this very morning, one of my Karsuk brutes has eaten up two entire birds'-nests, which I had just before gathered from the rocks.

"*August* 17.—In the afternoon came a gale from the southward. We had some rough rubbing from the floe-pieces, with three heavy hawsers out to the rocks of our little ice-breaker; but we held on. Toward midnight, our six-inch line, the smallest of the three, parted, but the other two held bravely. Feeling what good service this island has done us, what a Godsend it was to reach her, and how gallantly her broken rocks have protected us from the rolling masses of ice that grind by her, we have agreed to remember this anchorage as 'Godsend Ledge.'

"The walrus are very numerous, approaching within twenty feet of us, shaking their grim wet fronts, and mowing with their tusks the sea-ripples.

"*August* 19.—The walrus gather around us in crowds. I have always heard that the close approach to land of these sphinx-faced monsters portends a storm.

"*August* 20.—By Saturday morning it blew a perfect hurricane. We had seen it coming, and were ready with three good hawsers out ahead, and all things snug on board.

"Still it came on heavier and heavier, and the ice began to drive more wildly than I thought I had ever seen it. I had just turned in to warm and dry myself during a momentary lull, and was stretching myself out in my bunk, when I heard the sharp twanging snap of a cord. Our six-inch hawser had parted, and we were swinging by the two others, the gale roaring like a lion to the southward.

"Half a minute more, and 'twang, twang!' came a second report. I knew it was the whale-line by the shrillness of the ring. Our ten-inch cable still held on. I was hurrying my last sock into its seal-skin boot, when M'Gary came running down the companion-ladders:—'Captain Kane, she won't hold much longer; it's blowing the devil himself, and I am afraid to surge.'

"The cable was proving its excellence when I reached the deck; and the crew, as they gathered round me, were loud in its praises. We could hear its deep Æolian chant swelling through all the rattle of the running-gear and moaning of the shrouds. It was the death-song! The strands gave way with the noise of a shotted gun; and, in the smoke that followed their recoil, we were dragged out by the wild ice at its mercy.

"We steadied and did some petty warping, and got the brig a good bed in the rushing drift; but it all came to nothing. There was now but one thing left for us—to keep in some sort the command of the helm, by going freely where we must otherwise be driven.

"At seven in the morning we were close upon the piling masses. We dropped our heaviest anchor with the desperate hope of winding the brig; but there was no withstanding the ice torrent that followed us. We had only time to fasten a spar as a buoy to the chain, and let her slip. So went our best bower!

"Down we went upon the gale again, helplessly scraping along a lee of ice seldom less than thirty feet thick; one floe, measured by a line as we tried to fasten to it, more than forty. I had seen such ice only once before, but never in such rapid motion. One upturned mass rose above our gunwale, smashing in our bulwarks, and depositing half a ton of ice in a lump upon our decks. Our staunch little brig bore herself through all this wild adventure as if she had a charmed life.

"But a new enemy came in sight ahead. Directly in our way, just beyond the line of floe-ice against which we were alternately sliding and thumping, was a group of bergs. We had no power to avoid them; and the only question was, whether we were to be dashed in pieces against them, or whether they might not offer us some providential nook of refuge from the storm. But, as we neared them, we perceived that they were at some distance from the floe-edge, and separated from it by an interval of open water. Our hopes rose as the gale drove us toward this passage and into it; and we were ready to exult, when, from some unexplained cause,—probably an eddy of the wind against the lofty ice-walls,—we lost our headway. Almost at the same moment we saw that the bergs were not at rest; that with a momentum of their own they were bearing down upon the other ice, and that it must be our fate to be crushed between the two.

"Just then a broad low water-washed berg came driving up from the southward. The thought flashed upon me of one of our escapes in Melville Bay; and as the sconce moved rapidly close alongside us, M'Gary managed to plant an anchor on its slope and hold on to it by a whale-line. It was an anxious moment. Our noble tow-horse, whiter than the pale horse that seemed to be pursuing us, hauled us bravely on, the spray dashing over his windward flanks, and his forehead ploughing up the lesser ice as if in scorn. The bergs encroached upon us as we advanced; our channel narrowed to a width of perhaps forty feet; we braced the yards to clear the impending ice-walls.

"We passed clear; but it was a close shave,—so close that our port quarter-boat would have been crushed if we had not taken it in from the davits,—and found ourselves under the lee of a berg, in a comparatively open lead. Never did heart-tried men acknowledge with more gratitude their merciful deliverance from a wretched death.

"The day had already its full share of trials; but there were more to come. A flaw drove us from our shelter, and the gale soon carried us beyond the end of the lead. We were again in the ice, sometimes escaping its onset by warping, sometimes forced to rely on the strength and buoyancy of the brig to stand its pressure, sometimes scudding wildly through the half-open drift. Our jib-boom was snapped off; we carried away our barricade stanchions, and were forced to leave our little *Eric*,—as our life-boat was called,—with three brave fellows and their warps, out upon the floes behind us.

"A little pool of open water received us at last. It was just beyond a lofty cape that rose up like a wall, and under an iceberg that anchored itself between us and the gale. And here, close under the frowning shore of Greenland, ten miles nearer the Pole than our holding-ground of the morning, the men have turned in to rest.

"I was afraid to join them, for the gale was unbroken, and the floes kept pressing heavily upon our berg,—at one time so heavily as to sway it on its vertical axis toward the shore, and make its pinnacle overhang our vessel. My poor fellows had but a precarious sleep before our little harbour was broken up. They hardly reached the deck when we were driven astern, and our rudder splintered.

"Now began the nippings.* The first shock took us on our port-quarter, the brig bearing it well, and, after a moment of the old-fashioned suspense, rising by jerks handsomely. The next was from a veteran floe, tongued and honeycombed, but floating in a single table over twenty feet in thickness. Of course, no wood or iron could stand this; but the shore-ward face of our iceberg happened to present an inclined plane, descending deep into the water; and up this the brig was driven, as if some great power was forcing her into a dry dock.

"At one time I expected to see her carried bodily up its face and tumbled over on her side. But one of those mysterious relaxations, which I have elsewhere called the pulses of the ice, lowered us quite gradually down again into the rubbish, and we were forced out of the line of pressure toward the shore. Here we succeeded in carrying out a warp, and making fast. We grounded as the tide fell, and would have heeled over to seaward, but for a mass of detached land-ice that grounded alongside of us, and, although it stove our bulwarks as we rolled over it, shored us up."

I could hardly get to my bunk, as I went down into our littered cabin on the Sunday morning after our hard-working vigil of thirty-six hours. Bags of clothing, food, tents, India-rubber blankets, and the hundred little personal matters which every man likes to save in a time of trouble, were scattered around in places where the owners thought they might have them at hand. The pemmican had been

* *Nip*, the pressing in of ice round the vessel.

on deck, the boats equipped, and everything of real importance ready for a march, many hours before.

During the whole of the scenes I have been trying to describe, I could not help being struck by the composed and manly demeanour of my comrades. The turmoil of ice under a heavy sea often conveys the impression of danger when the reality is absent; but in this fearful passage, the parting of our hawsers, the loss of our anchors, the abrupt crushing of our stoven bulwarks, and the actual deposit of ice upon our decks, would have tried the nerves of the most experienced ice-men. All—officers and men —worked alike. Upon each occasion of collision with the ice which formed our lee-coast, efforts were made to carry out lines; and some narrow escapes were incurred by the zeal of the parties leading them into positions of danger. Mr Bonsall avoided being crushed by leaping to a floating fragment; and no less than four of our men at one time were carried down by the drift, and could only be recovered by a relief party after the gale had subsided.

It was not until the 22d that the storm abated, and our absent men were once more gathered back into their mess. During the interval of forced inaction, the little brig was fast to the ice-belt which lined the bottom of the cliffs, and all hands rested; but as soon as it was over, we took advantage of the flood-tide to pass our tow-lines to the ice-beach, and, harnessing ourselves in like mules on a canal, made a good three miles by tracking along the coast.

"*August* 23.—We tracked along the ice-belt for about one mile, when the tide fell, and the brig grounded, heeling over until she reached her bearings. She rose again at 10 P.M., and the crew turned out upon the ice-belt.

"*August* 24.—We have kept at it, tracking along, grounding at low water, but working like horses when the tides allowed us to move. We are now almost at the bottom of this indentation.

"We are sufficiently surrounded by ice to make our chances of escape next year uncertain, and yet not as far as I could wish for our spring journeys by the sledge.

"*August* 26.—My officers and crew are staunch and firm men; but the depressing influences of want of rest, the rapid advance of winter, and, above all, our slow progress, make them sympathize but little with this continued effort to force a way to the north. One of them, an excellent member of the party, volunteered an expression of opinion this morning in favour of returning to the south and giving up the attempt to winter."

It is unjust for a commander to measure his subordinates in such exigencies by his own standard. The interest which they feel in an undertaking is of a different nature from his own. With him there are always personal motives, apart from official duty, to stimulate effort. He receives, if successful, too large a share of the credit, and he justly bears all the odium of failure.

An apprehension—I hope a charitable one—of this fact leads me to consider the opinions of my officers with much respect. I called them together at once in a formal council, and listened to their views in full. With but one exception, Mr Henry Brooks, they were convinced that a further progress to the north was impossible, and were in favour of returning southward to winter.

Not being able conscientiously to take the same view, I explained to them the importance of securing a position which might expedite our sledge journeys in the future; and, after assuring them that such a position could only be attained by continuing our efforts, announced my intention of warping toward the northern headland of the bay,

"Once there, I shall be able to determine from actual inspection the best point for setting out on the operations of the spring; and at the nearest possible shelter to that point I will put the brig into winter harbour." My comrades received this decision in a manner that was most gratifying, and entered zealously upon the hard and cheerless duty it involved.

The warping began again, each man, myself included, taking his turn at the capstan. The ice seemed less heavy as we penetrated into the recess of the bay; our track-lines and shoulder-belts replaced the warps. Hot coffee was served out; and, in the midst of cheering songs, our little brig moved off briskly.

Our success, however, was not complete. At the very period of high-water she took the ground while close under the walls of the ice-foot. It would have been madness to attempt shoring her up. I could only fasten heavy tackle to the rocks which lined the base of the cliffs, and trust to the noble little craft's unassisted strength.

"*August* 27.—We failed, in spite of our efforts, to get the brig off with last night's tide; and, as our night-tides are generally the highest, I have some apprehensions as to her liberation.

"We have landed everything we could get upon the rocks, put out all our boats and filled them with portables alongside, sunk our rudder astern, and lowered our remaining heavy anchor into one of our quarter-boats. Heavy hawsers are out to a grounded lump of berg-ice, ready for instant heaving.

"Last night she heeled over again so abruptly that we were all tumbled out of our berths. At the same time the cabin stove, with a full charge of glowing anthracite,* was

* *Anthracite*, a hard coal found in America, which burns without smoke.

thrown down. The deck blazed smartly for a while; but, by sacrificing Mr Sontag's heavy pilot-cloth coat to the public good, I choked it down till water could be passed from above to extinguish it. It was fortunate we had water near at hand, for the powder was not far off.

"5 P.M. — She floats again, and our track-lines are manned. The men work with a will, and the brig moves along bravely.

"10 P.M.—Aground again; and the men, after a hot supper, have turned in to take a spell of sleep. The brig has a hard time of it with the rocks. She has been high and dry for each of the two last tides, and within three days has grounded no less than five times. I feel that this is hazardous navigation, but am convinced it is my duty to keep on. Except the loss of a portion of our false keel, we have sustained no real injury. The brig is still watertight, and her broken rudder and one shattered spar can be easily repaired.

"*August* 28.—By a complication of purchases, jumpers, and shores, we started the brig at 4 A.M.; and Mr Ohlsen having temporarily secured the rudder, I determined to enter the floe, and trust to the calm of the morning for a chance of penetrating to the northern land-ice ahead."

We had now a breathing spell, and I could find time to look out again upon the future. The broken and distorted area around us gave little promise of successful sledge-travel. But all this might change its aspect under the action of a single gale, and it was by no means certain that the ice-fields further north would have the same rugged and dispiriting character. Besides, the ice-belt was still before us, broken sometimes and difficult to traverse, but practicable for a party on foot, apparently for miles ahead; and I felt sure that a resolute boat's crew might push and track their way for some distance along it. I resolved to make the trial, and to judge what ought to be our wintering-ground from a personal inspection of the coast.

I had been quietly preparing for such an expedition for sometime. Our best and lightest whale-boat had been fitted with a canvas cover, that gave it all the comfort of a tent. We had a supply of pemmican ready packed in small cases, and a sledge taken to pieces was stowed away under the thwarts. In the morning of the 29th, Brooks, M'Gary, and myself, walked fourteen miles along the marginal ice; it was heavy and complicated with drift, but there was nothing about it to make me change my purpose.

My boat-crew consisted of seven, all of them volunteers and reliable:—Brooks, Bonsall, M'Gary, Sontag, Riley, Blake, and Morton. We had buffalo-robes for our sleeping-gear, and a single extra day suit was put on board as common property. Each man carried his girdle full of woollen socks, so as to dry them by the warmth of his body, and a tin cup, with a sheath-knife, at the belt; a soup-pot and lamp for the mess completed our outfit.

In less than three hours from my first order, the *Forlorn Hope* was ready for her work, covered with tin to prevent her being cut through by the bay-ice; and at half-past three in the afternoon she was freighted, launched, and on her way.

I placed Mr Ohlsen in command of the *Advance*, and Dr Hayes in charge of her log; Mr Ohlsen with orders to haul the brig to the southward and eastward into a safe berth, and there to await my return.

Many a warm shake of the hand from the men we left on board showed me that our good-bye was not a mere formality. Three hearty cheers from all hands followed us, —a Godspeed as we pushed off.

CHAPTER III.

OUR FIRST WALK OUT—THE DEPÔT PARTY.

In the first portions of our journey, we found a narrow but obstructed passage between the ice-belt and the outside pack. It was but a few yards in width, and the young ice upon it was nearly thick enough to bear our weight. By breaking it up we were able with effort to make about seven miles a day.

After such work,—wet, cold, and hungry,—the night's rest was very welcome. A couple of stanchions were rigged fore and aft, a sail tightly spread over the canvas cover of our boat, the cooking-lamp lit, and the buffalo-robes spread out. Dry socks replaced the wet, hot tea and pemmican followed, and very soon we forgot the discomforts of the day,—the smokers musing over their pipes, and the sleepers snoring in dreamless forgetfulness.

We had been out something less than twenty-four hours when we came to the end of our boating. In front and on one side was the pack, and on the other a wall some ten feet above our heads, the impracticable ice-belt. By waiting for high tide, and taking advantage of a chasm which a water-stream had worn in the ice, we managed to haul up our boat on its surface; but it was apparent that we must leave her there. She was stowed away snugly under the shelter of a large hummock;* and we pushed forward in our sledge, laden with a few articles of absolute necessity.

We had to pass our sledge carefully down large gorges in our path, winding occasionally and generally steep-

---

* *Hummock*, a ridge of broken ice.

Far North – Page 35.

sided, and bear it upon our shoulders, wading, of course, through water of an extremely low temperature. Our night halts were upon knolls of snow under the rocks. At one of these the tide overflowed our tent, and forced us to save our buffalo sleeping-gear by holding it up until the water subsided. This exercise, as it turned out, was more of a trial to our patience than to our health. The circulation was assisted perhaps by a perception of the ludicrous. Eight Yankee Caryatides, up to their knees in water, and an entablature sustaining such of their household gods as could not bear immersion!

On the 1st of September, still following the ice-belt, we found that we were entering the recesses of another bay but little smaller than that in which we had left our brig.

After an absence of five days, during which we made many scientific observations of great value, we found that we were but forty miles from the brig. Besides our small daily progress, we had lost much by the tortuous windings of the coast. The ice outside did not invite a change of plan in that direction; but I determined to leave the sledge and proceed overland on foot. With the exception of our instruments, we carried no weight but pemmican and one buffalo-robe. The weather, as yet not far below the freezing-point, did not make a tent essential to the bivouac; and, with this light equipment, we could travel readily two miles to one with our entire outfit. On the 4th of September we made twenty-four miles with comparative ease, and were refreshed by a comfortable sleep after the toils of the day.

The only drawback to this new method of advance was the inability to carry a sufficient quantity of food. Each man at starting had a fixed allowance of pemmican, which, with his other load, made an average weight of thirty-five pounds. It proved excessive; and we found—although we had good walkers in our party—that a very few pounds overweight broke us down.

Our progress on the 5th was arrested by another bay, much larger than any we had seen since entering Smith's Straits. It was a noble sheet of water, perfectly open, and thus in strange contrast to the ice outside. The cause of this, at the time inexplicable phenomenon, was found in a roaring and tumultuous river, which, issuing from a fiord at the inner sweep of the bay, rolled with the violence of a snow-torrent over a broken bed of rocks. This river, the largest probably yet known in North Greenland, was about three-quarters of a mile wide at its mouth, and admitted the tides for about three miles, when its bed rapidly ascended, and could be traced by the configuration of the hills as far as a large inner fiord. I called it Mary Minturn River, after the sister of Mrs Henry Grinnell. Its course was afterwards pursued to an interior glacier, from the base of which it was found to issue in numerous streams, that united into a single trunk about forty miles above its mouth. By the banks of this stream we encamped, lulled by the unusual music of running waters.

We forded our way across this river in the morning, carrying our pemmican as well as we could out of water, but submitting ourselves to a succession of plunge baths as often as we trusted our weight on the ice-capped stones above the surface. The average depth was not over our hips; but the crossing cost us so much labour, that we were willing to halt half a day to rest.

Leaving four of my party to recruit at this station, I started the next morning, with three volunteers, to cross the ice to the north-eastern headland, and thus save the almost impossible circuit by the shores of the bay.

We reached the headland after sixteen miles of walk, and found the ice-foot in good condition, evidently better fitted for sledge-travel than it was to the south. This point I named Cape William Makepeace Thackeray.

I now determined to seek some high headland beyond the cape, and make it my final point of reconnaissance.

I anxiously looked for, but could see no place combining so many of the requisites of a good winter harbour as the bay in which we left the *Advance*. Near its south-western corner the wide streams and the water-courses on the shore promised the earliest chances of liberation in the coming summer. It was secure against the moving ice: lofty headlands walled it in beautifully to seaward, enclosing an anchorage with a moderate depth of water; yet it was open to the meridian sunlight, and guarded from winds, eddies, and drift. The space enclosed was only occupied by a few rocky islets and our brig. We soon came in sight of her on our return march, as she lay at anchor in its southern sweep, with her masts cutting sharply against the white glacier; and, hurrying on through a gale, we were taken on board without accident.

My comrades gathered anxiously around me, waiting for the news. I told them in a few words of the results of our journey, and why I had determined upon remaining, and gave at once the order to warp in between the islands. We found seven-fathom soundings and a perfect shelter from the outside ice; and thus laid our little brig in the harbour, which we were fated never to leave together,—a long resting-place to her indeed, for the same ice is around her still.

The winter was now approaching rapidly. The thermometer had fallen by the 10th of September to 14°, and the young ice had cemented the floes so that we could walk and sledge round the brig. About sixty paces north of us an iceberg had been caught, and was frozen in; it was our neighbour while we remained in harbour. The rocky islets around us were fringed with hummocks; and, as the tide fell, their sides were coated with opaque crystals of bright white. The birds had gone.

"*September* 10.—We have plenty of responsible work before us. The long night 'when no man can work' is close at hand: in another month we shall lose the sun.

"First and foremost, we have to unstow the hold and deposit its contents in the storehouse on the shore. Brooks and a party are now briskly engaged in this double labour, running loaded boats along a canal that has to be recut every morning.

"Next comes the catering for winter diet. We have little or no game as yet in Smith's Sound; and, though the traces of deer that we have observed may be followed by the animals themselves, I cannot calculate upon them as a resource. Steaks of salt junk, artistically cut, are strung on lines and soaked in festoons under the ice. The salmon-trout and salt cod-fish which we bought at Fiskernaes are placed in barrels, perforated to permit a constant circulation of fresh water through them. Our pickled cabbage is similarly treated, after a little potash has been used to neutralize the acid. All these are submitted to twelve hours of alternate soaking and freezing, the crust of ice being removed from them before each immersion. This is the steward's province, and a most important one it is.

"Every one else is well employed,—M'Gary arranging and Bonsall making the inventory of our stores; Ohlsen and Petersen building our deck-house; while I am devising the plan of an architectural interior, which is to combine, of course, the utmost ventilation, room, dryness, warmth, general accommodation, comfort,—in a word, all the appliances of health.

"We have made a comfortable dog-house on the island; but they cannot be persuaded to sleep away from the vessel. They prefer the bare snow, where they can couch within the sound of our voices, to a warm kennel upon the rocks.

"*September* 11.—To-day came to us the first quiet Sunday of harbour life. We changed our log registration from sea-time to the familiar home series that begins at midnight. It is not only that the season has given us once more a local habitation; but there is something in the return of varying day and night that makes it grateful to reinstate this domestic observance. The long staring day, which has clung to us for more than two months, to the exclusion of the stars, has begun to intermit its brightness.

"We had our accustomed morning and evening prayers; and the day went by, full of sober thought, and, I trust, wise resolve.

"*September* 12.—Still going on with Saturday's operations, amid the thousand discomforts of house-cleaning and moving combined. I escaped them for an hour this morning, to fix with Mr Sontag upon a site for our observatory; and the men are already at work hauling the stone for it over the ice on sledges. It is to occupy a rocky islet, about a hundred yards off, that I have named after a little spot that I long to see again, 'FERN ROCK.' This is to be for me the centre of familiar localities. As the classic Mivins breakfasted lightly on a cigar, and took it out in sleep, so I have dined on salt pork and made my dessert of dreams.

"*September* 13.—Besides preparing our winter quarters, I am engaged in the preliminary arrangements for my provision-depôts along the Greenland coast. I purpose arranging three of them at intervals,—pushing them as far forward as I can,—to contain in all some twelve hundred pounds of provision, of which eight hundred will be pemmican."

My plans of future search were directly dependent upon the success of these operations of the autumn. With a chain of provision-depôts along the coast of Greenland, I could readily extend my travel by dogs. These noble animals formed the basis of my future plans: the only drawback to their efficiency as a means of travel was their inability to carry the heavy loads of provender essential for their support. A badly-fed or heavily-loaded dog is useless for a long journey; but with relays of provision, I could start empty, and fill up at our final station.

My dogs were both Esquimaux and Newfoundlanders. Of these last I had ten: they were to be carefully broken, to travel by voice without the whip, and were expected to be very useful for heavy draught, as their tractability would allow the driver to regulate their pace. I was already training them in a light sledge to drive, unlike the Esquimaux, two abreast, with a regular harness, a breast-collar of flat leather, and a pair of traces. Six of them made a powerful travelling-team; and four could carry me and my instruments, for short journeys around the brig, with great ease.

The sledge I used for them was built, with the care of cabinet-work, of American hickory, thoroughly seasoned. The runners were shod with annealed steel, and fastened by copper rivets, which could be renewed at pleasure. Except this, no metal entered into its construction. All its parts were held together by seal-skin lashings, so that it yielded to inequalities of surface and to sudden shock.

The three paramount considerations of lightness, strength, and diminished friction, were well combined in it. This beautiful, and, as we afterwards found, efficient and endurable sledge was named the *Little Willie*.

The Esquimaux dogs were reserved for the great tug of the actual journeys of search. They were now in the semi-savage condition which marks their close approach to the wolf; and, according to Mr Petersen, under whose care they were placed, were totally useless for journeys over such ice as was now before us. A hard experience had not then opened my eyes to the inestimable value of these dogs: I had yet to learn their power and speed, their patient, enduring fortitude, their sagacity in tracking these icy morasses, among which they had been born and bred.

The men appointed to establish the depôt were furnished with a sledge. Its model—which had been previously tested by the adventurous journeys of M'Clintock in Lancaster Sound—was to lessen the height and somewhat increase the breadth of the runner; both of which, I think, were improvements, giving increased strength. I named her the *Faith*. Her length was thirteen feet, and breadth four. She could readily carry fourteen hundred pounds of mixed stores.

This noble old sledge, which is now endeared to me by every pleasant association, bore the brunt of the heaviest parties, and came back, after the descent of the coast, comparatively sound. The men were attached in her in such a way as to make the line of draught or traction as near as possible in the axis of the weight. Each man had his own shoulder-belt, or "rue-raddy," as we used to call it, and his own track-line, which, for want of horse-hair, was made of Manilla rope; it traversed freely by a ring on a loop or bridle, that extended from runner to runner in front of the sledge.

The cargo for this journey, without including the provisions of the party, was almost exclusively pemmican. Some of this was put up in cylinders of tinned iron with conical terminations, so as to resist the assaults of the white bear; but the larger quantity was in strong wooden cases or kegs, well hooped with iron, holding about seventy pounds each. Surmounting this load was a light India-rubber boat, made quite portable by a frame of basket-willow, which I hoped to launch on reaching the open water.

The personal equipment of the men was a buffalo-robe for the party to lie upon, and a bag of Mackinaw blanket for each man to crawl into at night. India-rubber cloth was to be the protection from the snow beneath. The tent was of canvas, made after the plan of our English predecessors. We afterward learned to modify and reduce our travelling gear, and found that in direct proportion to its simplicity and our apparent privation of articles of supposed necessity, were our actual comfort and practical efficiency. Step by step, as long as our Arctic service continued, we went on reducing our sledging outfit, until at last we came to the Esquimaux ultimatum of simplicity —raw meat and a fur bag.

"*September* 20.—I was unwilling to delay my depôt party any longer. M'Gary and Bonsall, with five men., left the brig at half-past one to-day. We gave them three cheers, and I accompanied them with my dogs, as a farewell escort, for some miles.

"Our crew proper is now reduced to three men; but all the officers, the doctor among the rest, are hard at work upon the observatory and its arrangements."

CHAPTER IV.

DOMESTIC TROUBLES—RETURN OF THE DEPÔT PARTY.

The island on which we placed our observatory was some fifty paces long by perhaps forty broad, and about thirty feet above the water-line. Here we mounted our transit and theodolite.

The magnetic observatory adjoined, and had rather more of the affectation of comfort. No iron was used in its construction. Here were our magnetometer and dip instruments; and the tide-register was placed on board the vessel.

Our meteorological observatory was upon the open icefield, one hundred and forty yards from the ship. It was a wooden structure, latticed and pierced with augur-holes on all sides, so as to allow the air to pass freely, and firmly luted to its frozen base. This was well supplied with thermometers of all varieties.

"*September* 30.—We have been terribly annoyed by rats. Some days ago we made a brave effort to smoke them out with the vilest imaginable compound of vapours,—brimstone, burnt leather, and arsenic,—and spent a cold night in a deck-bivouac, to give the experiment fair play. But they survived the fumigation. We now determined to dose them with carbonic acid gas. Dr Hayes burnt a quantity of charcoal; and we shut down the hatches, after closing up every fissure that communicated aft, and starting three stoves on the skin of the forepeak.

"As the gas was generated with extreme rapidity in the confined area below, great caution had to be exercised.

Our French cook, good Pierre Schubert,—who to a considerable share of bull-headed intrepidity unites a commendable portion of professional zeal,—stole below, without my knowledge or consent, to season a soup. Morton fortunately saw him staggering in the dark, and, reaching him with great difficulty as he fell, both were hauled up in the end,—Morton, his strength almost gone, and the cook perfectly insensible.

"The next disaster was of a graver sort. I record it with emotions of mingled awe and thankfulness. We have narrowly escaped being burnt out of house and home. I had given orders that the fires, lit under my own eye, should be regularly inspected; but I learned that Pierre's misadventure had made the watch pretermit for a time opening the hatches. As I lowered a lantern, which was extinguished instantly, a suspicious odour reached me, as of burning wood. I descended at once. Reaching the deck of the forecastle, my first glance toward the fires showed me that all was safe there; and, though the quantity of smoke still surprised me, I was disposed to attribute it to the recent kindling. But at this moment, while passing on my return near the door of the bulkhead, which leads to the carpenter's room, the gas began to affect me. My lantern went out as if quenched by water; and, as I ran by the bulkhead door, I saw the deck near it a mass of glowing fire for some three feet in diameter. I could not tell how much further it extended, for I became quite insensible at the foot of the ladder, and would have sunk, had not Mr Brooks seen my condition and hauled me out.

"When I came to myself, which happily was very soon, I confided my fearful secret to the four men around me, Brooks, Ohlsen, Blake, and Stevenson. It was all-important to avoid confusion: we shut the doors of the galley, so as to confine the rest of the crew and officers aft, and then passed up water from the fire-hole alongside. It was all done very quietly. Ohlsen and myself went down to the burning deck; Brooks handed us in the buckets; and in less than ten minutes we were in safety. We found the fire had originated in the remains of a barrel of charcoal, which had been left in the carpenter's room, ten feet from the stoves, and with a bulkhead separating it from them. How it had been ignited it was impossible to know. Our safety was due to the dense charge of carbonic acid gas which surrounded the fire, and the exclusion of atmospheric air. When the hatches were opened the flame burst out with energy. Our fire-hole was invaluable; and I rejoiced that, in the midst of our heavy duties, this essential of an Arctic winter harbour had not been neglected. The ice around the brig was already fourteen inches thick.

"*October* 1.—Upon inspecting the scene of yesterday's operations, we found twenty-eight well-fed rats of all varieties of age. The cook, though unable to do duty, is better; I can hear him chanting his Béranger through the blankets in his bunk.

"*October* 3.—On shore to the south-east, above the first terrace, Mr Petersen found unmistakable signs of a sledge-passage. The tracks were deeply impressed, but certainly more than one season old. This adds to our hope that the natives, whose ancient traces we saw on the point south of Godsend Ledge, may return this winter.

"*October* 5.—A circumstance that happened to-day is of serious concern to us. Our dogs have been adding to our stock. We have now on hand four reserved puppies of peculiar promise; six have been ignominiously drowned, two devoted to a pair of mittens for Dr Kane, and seven eaten by their mammas. Yesterday the mother of one batch, a pair of fine white pups, showed peculiar symptoms. We recalled the fact that for days she had avoided water, or had drunk with spasms and evident aversion; but hydrophobia, which is unknown north of 70°, never occurred to us. The animal was noticed this morning walking up and down the deck with a staggering gait, her head depressed, and her mouth frothing and tumid. Finally she snapped at Petersen, and fell foaming and biting at his feet. He reluctantly pronounced it hydrophobia, and advised me to shoot her. The advice was well-timed: I had hardly cleared the deck before she snapped at Hans, the Esquimaux, and recommenced her walking trot. It was quite an anxious moment to me; for my Newfoundlanders were around the housing, and the hatches open. We shot her, of course.

"*October* 8.—I have been practising with my dog-sledge and an Esquimaux team till my arms ache. To drive such an equipage, a certain proficiency with the whip is indispensable; which, like all proficiency, must be worked for. In fact, the weapon has an exercise of its own, quite peculiar, and is as hard to learn as single-stick or broadsword.

"*October* 10.—Our depôt party has been out twenty days, and it is time they were back: their provisions must have run very low, for I enjoined them to leave every pound at the depôt they could spare. I am going out with supplies to look after them. I take four of our best Newfoundlanders, now well broken, in our lightest sledge; and Blake will accompany me with his skates. We have not hands enough to equip a sledge party, and the ice is too unsound for us to attempt to ride with a large team."

My first effort was, of course, to reach the land; but it was unfortunately low tide, and the ice-belt rose up before me like a wall. The pack was becoming more and more unsafe, and I was extremely anxious to gain an asylum on shore; for, though it was easy to find a temporary refuge by retreating to the old floes which studded the more recent ice, I knew that in doing so we should risk being carried down by the drift.

The dogs began to flag; but we had to press them;—we were only two men; and, in the event of the animals failing to leap any of the rapidly-multiplying fissures, we could hardly expect to extricate our laden sledge. Three times, in less than three hours, my shaft or hinder dogs went in; and John and myself, who had been trotting alongside the sledge for sixteen miles were nearly as tired as they were. This state of things could not last; and I therefore made for the old ice to sea-ward.

We were nearing it rapidly, when the dogs failed in leaping a chasm that was somewhat wider than the others and the whole concern came down in the water. I cut the lines instantly, and, with the aid of my companion, hauled the poor animals out. We owed the preservation of the sledge to their admirable docility and perseverance. The tin-cooking apparatus and the air confined in the India-rubber coverings kept it afloat till we could succeed in fastening a couple of seal-skin cords to the cross-pieces at the front and back. By these John and myself were able to give it an uncertain support from the two edges of the opening, till the dogs, after many fruitless struggles, carried it forward at last upon the ice.

Although the thermometer was below zero, and in our wet state we ran a considerable risk of freezing, the urgency of our position left no room for thoughts of cold. We started at a run, men and dogs, for the solid ice; and by the time we had gained it we were steaming in the cold atmosphere like a couple of vapour-baths.

We rested on the floe. We could not raise our tent, for it had frozen hard. But our buffalo-robe bags gave us protection; and, though we were too wet inside to be absolutely comfortable, we managed to get something like sleep before it was light enough for us to move on again.

The journey was continued in the same way for a few days; but we found, to our great gratification, that the cracks closed with the change of the tide, and at high-water we succeeded in gaining the ice-belt under the cliffs.

Our progress averaged twenty miles a day since leaving the brig, and we were within a short march of the cape which I have named William Wood, when a broad chasm brought us to a halt. It was in vain that we worked out to sea-ward, or dived into the shore-ward recesses of the bay: the ice everywhere presented the same impassable fissures. We had no alternative but to retrace our steps and seek among the bergs some place of security. We found a camp for the night on the old floe-ices to the westward, gaining them some time after the darkness had closed in.

On the morning of the 15th, about two hours before the late sunrise, as I was preparing to climb a berg from which I might have a sight of the road ahead, I perceived far off upon the white snow a dark object, which not only moved, but altered its shape strangely,—now expanding into a long black line, now waving, now gathering itself up into a compact mass. It was the returning sledge party. They had seen our black tent, and ferried across to seek it.

They were most welcome; for their absence, in the fearfully open state of the ice, had filled me with apprehensions. We could not distinguish each other as we drew near in the twilight; and my first good news of them was when I heard that they were singing. On they came, and at last I was able to count their voices, one by one. Thank God, seven! Poor John Blake was so breathless with gratulation, that I could not get him to blow his signal-horn. We gave them, instead, the good old English greeting, " three cheers!" and in a few minutes were among them.

They had made a creditable journey, and were, on the whole, in good condition. They had no injuries worth talking about, although not a man had escaped some touches of the frost. Bonsall was *minus* a big toe-nail, and *plus* a scar upon the nose. M'Gary had attempted, as Tom Hickey had told us, to *pluck* a fox, it being so frozen as to defy skinning by his knife; and his fingers had been tolerably frost-bitten in the operation. "They're very horny, sir, are my fingers," said M'Gary, who was worn down to a mere shadow of his former rotundity; "very horny, and they water up like bladders." The rest had suffered in their feet; but, like good fellows, postponed limping until they reached the ship.

Within the last three days they had marched fifty-four miles. Their sledge being empty, and the young ice north of Cape Bancroft smooth as a mirror, they had travelled, the day before we met them, nearly twenty-five miles. A very remarkable pace for men who had been twenty-eight days in the field.

My supplies of hot food, coffee, and marled beef soup, which I had brought with me, were very opportune. They had almost exhausted their bread; and, being unwilling to encroach on the depôt stores, had gone without fuel in order to save alcohol. Leaving orders to place my own sledge stores in *cache*, I returned to the brig, ahead of the party, with my dog-sledge, carrying Mr Bonsall with me.

This extract from the journal shows how the men fared on reaching the brig:—" The spar-deck—or, as we call it from its wooden covering, the ' house'—is steaming with the buffalo robes, tents, boots, socks, and heterogeneous costumings of our returned parties. We have ample work in repairing these and restoring the disturbed order of our domestic life. The men feel the effects of their journey, but are very content in their comfortable quarters. A pack of cards, grog at dinner, and the promise of a three days' holiday, have made the decks happy with idleness and laughter."

CHAPTER V.

OUR FIRST WINTER.

"*November* 7.—The darkness is coming on with insidious steadiness, and its advances can only be perceived by comparing one day with its fellow of some time back.

"Except upon the island of Spitzbergen, which has the advantages of an insular climate and tempered by ocean currents, no Christians have wintered in so high a latitude as this. They are Russian sailors who make the encounter there, men inured to hardships and cold.

"*November* 9.—Wishing to get the altitude of the cliffs on the south-west cape of our bay before the darkness set in thoroughly, I started in time to reach them with my Newfoundlanders at noonday. Although it was but a short journey, the rough shore-ice and a slight wind rendered the cold severe. I had been housed for a week with my wretched rheumatism, and felt that daily exposure was necessary to enable me to bear up against the cold. The thermometer indicated 23° below zero

"*November* 16.—The great difficulty is to keep up a cheery tone among the men. Poor Hans has been sorely home-sick. Three days ago he bundled up his clothes and took his rifle, to bid us all good-bye. It turns out that besides his mother there is another of the softer sex at Fiskernaes that the boy's heart is dreaming of. He looked as wretched as any lover of a milder clime. I hope I have treated his nostalgia successfully, by giving him first a dose of salts, and secondly, promotion. He has now all the dignity of a henchman. He harnesses my dogs, builds my traps, and walks with me on my ice-tramps; and, except hunting, is excused from all other duty. He is really attached to me, and as happy as a fat man ought to be.

"*November* 22.—I offered a prize to-day of a Guernsey shirt to the man who held out longest in a 'fox chase' round the decks. The rule of the sport was, that 'Fox' was to run a given circuit between galley and capstan, all hands following on his track; every four minutes a halt to be called to blow, and the fox making the longest run to take the prize; each of the crew to run as fox in turn. William Godfrey sustained the chase for fourteen minutes, and *wore* off the shirt.

"*November* 27.—I sent out a volunteer party some days ago with Mr Bonsall, to see whether the Esquimaux have returned to the huts we saw empty at the cape. The thermometer was in the neighbourhood of 40° below zero, and the day was too dark to read at noon. I was hardly surprised when they returned after camping one night upon the snow. Their sledge broke down, and they were obliged to leave tents and everything else behind them. It must have been very cold, for a bottle of Monongahela whisky of good stiff proof froze under Mr Bonsall's head.

"Morton went out on Friday to reclaim the things they

had left, and to-day at 1 P.M. he returned successful. He reached the wreck of the former party, making nine miles in three hours,—pushed on six miles further on the ice-foot,—then camped for the night; and, making a sturdy march the next day without luggage, reached the huts, and got back to his camp to sleep. This journey of his was, we then thought, really an achievement,—sixty-two miles in three marches, with a mean temperature of 40° below zero, and a noonday so dark that you could hardly see a hummock of ice fifty paces ahead.

" Under more favouring circumstances, Bonsall, Morton, and myself made eighty-four miles in three consecutive marches. I go for the system of forced marches on journeys that are not over a hundred and fifty miles. A practised walker unencumbered by weight does twenty miles a day nearly as easily as ten: it is the uncomfortable sleeping that wears a party out.

" *December* 12.—A grand incident in our great monotony of life! We had an occultation of Saturn at 2 A.M., and got a most satisfactory observation. The emersion was obtained with greater accuracy than could have been expected from the excessive atmospheric undulation of these low temperatures. My little Fraunhöfer sustained its reputation well. We can now fix our position without a cavil.

" *December* 15.—We have lost the last vestige of our mid-day twilight. We cannot see print, and hardly paper the fingers cannot be counted a foot from the eyes. Noonday and midnight are alike, and, except a vague glimmer on the sky that seems to define the hill outlines to the south, we have nothing to tell us that this Arctic world of ours has a sun. In one week more we shall reach the midnight of the year.

"*December* 22.—There is an excitement in our little community that dispenses with reflections upon the solstitial night. 'Old Grim' is missing, and has been for more than a day. Since the lamented demise of Cerberus, my leading Newfoundlander, he has been patriarch of our scanty kennel.

"Old Grim was a 'character' such as peradventure may at some time be found among beings of a higher order and under a more temperate sky. A profound hypocrite and time-server, he so wriggled his adulatory tail as to secure every one's good graces and nobody's respect. All the spare morsels, the cast-off delicacies of the mess, passed through the winnowing jaws of 'Old Grim,'—an illustration not so much of his eclecticism as his universality of taste. He was never known to refuse anything offered or approachable, and never known to be satisfied, however prolonged and abundant the bounty or the spoil.

"Grim was an ancient dog: his teeth indicated many winters; and his limbs, once splendid tractors for the sledge, were now covered with warts and ringbones. Somehow or other, when the dogs were harnessing for a journey, 'Old Grim' was sure not to be found; and upon one occasion, when he was detected hiding away in a cast-off barrel, he incontinently became lame. Strange to say, he has been lame ever since, except when the team is away without him.

"Cold disagrees with Grim; but by a system of patient watchings at the door of our deck-house, accompanied by a discriminating use of his tail, he became at last the one privileged intruder. My seal-skin coat has been his favourite bed for weeks together. Whatever love for an individual Grim expressed by his tail, he could never be induced to follow him on the ice after the cold darkness of the winter set in; yet the dear, good old sinner would wriggle after you to the very threshold of the gangway, and bid you good-bye with a deprecatory wag of the tail which disarmed resentment.

"His appearance was quite characteristic: his muzzle roofed like the old-fashioned gable of a Dutch garret-window; his forehead indicating the most meagre capacity of brains that could consist with his sanity as a dog; his eyes small, his mouth curtained by long black dewlaps, and his hide a mangy russet studded with chestnut-burrs; if he has gone indeed, we 'ne'er shall look upon his like again.' So much for old Grim!

"When yesterday's party started to take soundings, I thought the exercise would benefit Grim, whose time-serving sojourn on our warm deck had begun to render him over-corpulent. A rope was fastened round him, for at such critical periods he was obstinate, and even ferocious; and, thus fastened to the sledge, he commenced his reluctant journey. Reaching a stopping-place after a while, he jerked upon his line, parted it a foot or two from its knot, and, dragging the remnant behind him, started off through the darkness in the direction of our brig. He has not been seen since.

"*December* 23.—Our anxieties for old Grim might have interfered with almost anything else; but they could not arrest our celebration of yesterday. Dr Hayes made us a well-studied oration, and Morton a capital punch; add to these a dinner of marled beef,—we have two pieces left, for the sun's return and the 4th of July,—and a bumper of champagne all round; and the elements of our frolic are all registered.

"We tracked old Grim to-day through the snow to within six hundred yards of the brig, and thence to that mass of snow-packed sterility which we call the shore. His not rejoining the ship is a mystery quite in keeping with his character."

My journal for the first two months of 1854 is so devoid of interest, that I spare the reader the task of following me through it. In the darkness and consequent inaction, as it was almost in vain that we sought to create topics of thought, and by a forced excitement to ward off the encroachments of disease. Our observatory and the dogs gave us our only regular occupations.

The first traces of returning light were observed at noon on the 21st of January, when the southern horizon had for a short time a distinct orange tint. Though the sun had perhaps given us a band of illumination before, it was not distinguishable from the cold light of the planets.

The influence of this long, intense darkness was most depressing. Even our dogs, although the greater part of them were natives of the Arctic Circle, were unable to withstand it. Most of them died from an anomalous form of disease, to which, I am satisfied, the absence of light contributed as much as the extreme cold. I give a little extract from my journal of January 20:—

"This morning at five o'clock—for I am so afflicted with the insomnium of this eternal night, that I rise at any time between midnight and noon—I went upon deck. It was absolutely dark; the cold not permitting a swinging lamp. There was not a glimmer came to me through the ice-crusted window-panes of the cabin. While I was feeling my way, half puzzled as to the best method of steering clear of whatever might be before me, two of my Newfoundland dogs put their cold noses against my hand, and instantly commenced the most exuberant antics of satisfaction. It then occurred to me how very dreary and forlorn must these poor animals be, at atmospheres 10° indoors and 50° without,—living in darkness, howling at an accidental light, as if it reminded them of the moon,—and with nothing, either of instinct or sensation, to tell them of the passing hours, or to explain the long-lost daylight. They shall see the lanterns more frequently.

"*January* 25.—The mouse-coloured dogs, the leaders of my Newfoundland team, have for the past fortnight been nursed like babies. No one can tell how anxiously I watch them. They are kept below, tended, fed, cleansed, caressed, and *doctored*, to the infinite discomfort of all hands. To-day I give up the last hope of saving them. Their disease is as clearly mental as in the case of any human being. The more material functions of the poor brutes go on without interruption : they eat voraciously, retain their strength, and sleep well. But all the indications beyond this go to prove that the original epilepsy, which was the first manifestation of brain disease among them, has been followed by a true lunacy. They bark frenziedly at nothing, and walk in straight and curved lines with anxious and unwearying perseverance."

On the 22d, I took my first walk on the great floe, which had been so long a time a crude, black labyrinth. I give the appearance of things in the words of my journal :—

"The floe has changed wonderfully. I remember it sixty-four days ago, when our twilight was as it now is, a partially snow-patched plain, chequered with ridges of sharp hummocks, or a series of long icy levels, over which I coursed with my Newfoundlanders. All this has gone. A lead-coloured expanse stretches its 'rounding grey' in every direction, and the old angular hummocks are so softened down as to blend in rolling dunes with distant obscurity. The snow upon the levels shows the same remarkable evaporation. It is now in crisp layers, hardly six inches thick, quite undisturbed by drift. I could hardly recognise any of the old localities."

I close my notice of these dreary months with a single extract more. The date of it is February 21st.

"We have had the sun for some days silvering the ice between the headlands of the bay; and to-day, toward noon, I started out to be the first of my party to welcome him back. It was the longest walk and toughest climb that I have had since our imprisonment; and scurvy and general debility have made me 'short o' wind.' But I managed to attain my object. I saw him once more; and upon a projecting crag nestled in the sunshine. It was like bathing in perfumed water."

The month of March brought back to us the perpetual day. The sunshine had reached our deck on the last day of February; we needed it to cheer us. We were not as pale as my experience in Lancaster Sound had foretold, but the scurvy-spots that mottled our faces gave sore proof of the trials we had undergone. It was plain that we were all of us unfit for arduous travel on foot at the intense temperatures of the nominal spring; and the return of the sun, by increasing the evaporation from the floes, threatened us with a recurrence of still severer weather.

But I felt that our work was unfinished. The great object of the expedition challenged us to a more northward exploration. My dogs, that I had counted on so largely, the nine splendid Newfoundlanders and thirty-five Esquimaux of six months before, had perished; there were only six survivors of the whole pack, and one of these was unfit for draught. Still, they formed my principal reliance, and I busied myself from the very beginning of the month in training them to run together. The carpenter was set to work upon a small sledge, on an improved model, and adapted to the reduced force of our team ; and, as we had exhausted our stock of small cord to lash its parts together, Mr Brooks rigged up a miniature rope-walk, and was preparing a new supply from part of the material of our deep-sea lines. The operations of shipboard, however, went on regularly; Hans, and occasionally Petersen, going out on the hunt, though rarely returning successful.

The reader may be disposed to wonder how we got through our long dark night. It was certainly very dull; and the following account of one day will convey a very good idea of the whole season :—

"At six in the morning M'Gary is called, with all hands who have *slept in*. The decks are cleaned, the ice-hole opened, the refreshing beef-nets examined, the ice-tables measured, and things aboard put to rights. At half-past seven all hands rise, wash on deck, open the doors for ventilation, and come below for breakfast. We are short of fuel and therefore cook in the cabin. Our breakfast, for all fare alike, is hard tack, pork, stewed apples frozen like molasses-candy, tea and coffee, with a delicate portion of raw potato. After breakfast the smokers take their pipe till nine; then all hands turn to, idlers to idle and workers to work; Ohlsen to his bench, Brooks to his 'preparations' in canvas, M'Gary to play tailor, Whipple to make shoes, Bonsall to tinker, Baker to skin birds, and the rest to the 'Office!' Take a look into the Arctic bureau! One table, one salt-pork lamp with rusty chlorinated flame, three stools, and as many waxen-faced men with their legs drawn up under them, the deck at zero being too cold for the feet. Each has his department: Kane is writing, sketching, and projecting maps; Hayes copying logs and meteorologicals; Sontag reducing his work at Fern Rock.

A fourth, as one of the working members of the hive, has long been defunct; you will find him in bed. At twelve a business round of inspection, and orders enough to fill up the day with work. Next, the drill of the Esquimaux dogs—my own peculiar recreation—a dog-trot specially refreshing to legs that creak with every kick, and rheumatic shoulders that chronicle every descent of the whip. And so we get on to dinner-time—the occasion of another gathering, which misses the tea and coffee of breakfast, but rejoices in pickled cabbage and dried peaches instead.

"At dinner, as at breakfast, the raw potato comes in, our hygienic luxury. Like doctor-stuff generally, it is not as appetising as desirable. Grating it down nicely, leaving out the ugly red spots liberally, and adding the utmost oil as a lubricant, it is as much as I can do to persuade the mess to shut their eyes and bolt it, like Mrs Squeers' molasses and brimstone at Dotheboys Hall. Two absolutely refuse to taste it. I tell them of the Silesians using its leaves as spinach, of the whalers in the South Seas getting drunk on the molasses which had preserved the large potatoes of the Azores—I point to this gum, so fungoid and angry the day before yesterday, and so flat and amiable to-day—all by a potato poultice; my eloquence is wasted; they persevere in rejecting the admirable compound.

"Sleep, exercise, amusement, and work at will, carry on the day till our six o'clock supper, a meal something like breakfast and something like dinner, only a little more scant; and the officers come in with the reports of the day. Dr Hayes shows me the log, I sign it; Sontag the weather, I sign the weather; Mr Bonsall the tides and thermometers. Thereupon comes in mine ancient, Brooks; and I enter in his journal all the work done under his charge, and discuss his labours for the morrow.

" M'Gary comes next, with the cleaning-up arrangement, inside, outside, and on decks; and Mr Wilson follows with ice-measurements. And last of all comes my own record of the day gone by; every line, as I look back upon its pages, giving evidence of a weakened body and harassed mind."

Meanwhile we talked encouragingly of spring hopes and summer prospects, and managed sometimes to force an occasion for mirth out of the very discomforts of our unyielding winter life.

This may explain the tone of my diary.

CHAPTER VI.

AN ANXIOUS SEARCH.

" Not a man now, except Pierre and Morton, is exempt from scurvy; and, as I look around upon the pale faces and haggard looks of my comrades, I feel that we are fighting the battle of life at disadvantage, and that an Arctic night and an Arctic day age a man more rapidly and harshly than a year anywhere else in all this weary world.

" *March* 13.—Since January, we have been working at the sledges and other preparations for travel. The death of my dogs, the rugged obstacles of the ice, and the intense cold, have obliged me to reorganise our whole equipment. We have had to discard all our India-rubber fancy-work;

canvas shoe-making, fur-socking, sewing, carpentering, are all going on; and the cabin, our only fire-warmed apartment, is the workshop, kitchen, parlour, and hall. Pemmican cases are thawing on the lockers; buffalo-robes are drying around the stove; camp equipments occupy the corners; and our woe-begone French cook, with an infinitude of useless saucepans, insists on monopolising the stove.

"*March* 17.—It is nine o'clock P.M., and the thermometer outside at — 46°. I am anxious to have my depôt party off; but I must wait until there is a promise of milder weather. It must come soon. The sun is almost at the equator. On deck, I can see to the northward all the bright glare of sunset, streaming out in long bands of orange through the vapours of the ice-foot, and the frost-smoke exhaling in wreaths like those from the house-chimneys a man sees in the valleys as he comes down a mountain side.

"*March* 18.—To-day our spring-tides gave to the massive ice which sustains our little vessel a rise and fall of seventeen feet. The crunching and grinding, the dashing of the water, the gurgling of the eddies, and the toppling over of the nicely-poised ice-tables, were unlike the more brisk dynamics of hummock action, but conveyed a more striking expression of power and dimension.

"The thermometer at four o'clock in the morning was — 49°; too cold still, I fear, for our sledgemen to set out. But we packed the sledge and strapped on the boat, and determined to see how she would drag. Eight men attached themselves to the lines, but were scarcely able to move her. This may be due in part to an increase of friction produced by the excessive cold, according to the experience of the Siberian travellers; but I have no doubt it is principally caused by the very thin runners of our Esquimaux sledge cutting through the snow-crust.

"The excessive refraction this evening, which entirely lifted up the northern coast as well as the icebergs, seems to give the promise of milder weather. In the hope that it may be so, I have fixed on to-morrow for the departure of the sledge, after very reluctantly dispensing with more than two hundred pounds of her cargo, besides the boat. The party think they can get along with it now.

"*March* 20.—I saw the depôt party off yesterday. They gave the usual three cheers, with three for myself. I gave them the whole of my brother's great wedding-cake and my last two bottles of Port, and they pulled the sledge they were harnessed to famously. But I was not satisfied. I could see it was hard work; and, besides, they were without the boat, or enough extra pemmican to make their deposit of importance. I followed them, therefore, and found that they encamped at 8 P.M. only five miles from the brig.

"When I overtook them I said nothing to discourage them, and gave no new orders for the morning; but after laughing at good Ohlsen's rueful face, and listening to all Petersen's assurances that the cold and nothing but the cold retarded his Greenland sledge, and that no sledge of any other construction could have been moved at all through — 40° snow, I quietly bade them good-night, leaving all hands under their buffaloes.

"Once returned to the brig, all my tired remainder-men were summoned; a large sled with broad runners, which I had built somewhat after the neat Admiralty model sent me by Sir Francis Beaufort, was taken down, scraped, polished, lashed, and fitted with track-ropes and *rue-raddies* —the lines arranged to draw as near as possible in a line with the centre of gravity. We made an entire cover of canvas, with snugly-adjusted fastenings; and by one in the morning we had our discarded excess of pemmican and the boat once more in stowage.

"Off we went for the camp of the sleepers. It was very cold, but a thoroughly Arctic night—the snow just tinged with the crimson stratus above the sun, which, equinoctial as it was, glared beneath the northern horizon like a smelting-furnace. We found the tent of the party by the bearings of the stranded bergs. Quietly and stealthily we hauled away their Esquimaux sledge, and placed her cargo upon the *Faith*. Five men were then 'rue-raddied' to the track-lines, and with the whispered word, 'Now, boys, when Mr Brooks gives his third snore, off with you!' off they went, and the *Faith* after them, as free and nimble as a volunteer. The trial was a triumph. We awakened the sleepers with three cheers; and, giving them a second good-bye, returned to the brig, carrying the dishonoured vehicle along with us. And now, barring mishaps past anticipation, I shall have a depôt for my long trip.

"The party were seen by M'Gary from aloft, at noon to-day, moving easily, and about twelve miles from the brig. The temperature too is rising, or rather unmistakably about to rise. Our lowest was — 43°, but our highest reached — 22°; this extreme range, with the excessive refraction and a gentle misty air from about the south-east, makes me hope that we are going to have a warm spell. The party is well off. Now for my own to follow them.

"*March* 21.—All hands at work house-cleaning. Thermometer — 48°. Visited the fox-traps with Hans in the afternoon, and found one poor animal frozen dead. A hard thing about his fate was that he had succeeded in effecting his escape from the trap, but, while working his way underneath, had been frozen fast to a smooth stone by the moisture of his own breath. He was not probably aware of it before the moment when he sought to avail himself of his hard-gained liberty. These saddening thoughts did not impair my appetite at supper, where the little creature looked handsomer than ever.

"*March* 22.—We took down the forward bulkhead to-day, and moved the men aft, to save fuel. All hands are still at work clearing up the decks, the scrapers sounding overhead, and the hickory-brooms crackling against the frozen woodwork. Afternoon comes, and M'Gary brings from the traps two foxes, a blue and a white. Afternoon passes, and we skin them. Evening passes, and we eat them. Never were foxes more welcome visitors, or treated more like domestic animals.

"*March* 27.—We have been for some days in all the flurry of preparation for our exploration trip: buffalo-hides, leather, and tailoring utensils everywhere. Every particle of fur comes in play for mits, and muffs, and wrappers. Poor Flora is turned into a pair of socks, and looks almost as pretty as when she was heading the team.

"The wind to-day made it intensely cold. In riding but four miles to inspect a fox-trap, the movement froze my cheeks twice. We avoid masks with great care, reserving them for the severer weather; the jaw when protected recovers very soon the sensibility which exposure has subdued.

"*March* 31.—I was within an ace to-day of losing my dogs, every one of them. When I reached the ice-foot, they balked;—who would not?—the tide was low, the ice rampant, and a jump of four feet necessary to reach the crest. The howling of the wind and the whirl of the snow-drift confused the poor creatures; but it was valuable training for them, and I strove to force them over. Of course I was on foot, and they had a light load behind them. 'Now, Stumpy! Now, Whitey!' 'Good dogs!' 'Tu-lee-ēē-ēē! Tuh!' They went at it like good staunch brutes, and the next minute the whole team was rolling in a lump, some sixteen feet below me, in the chasm of the ice-foot. The drift was such that at first I could not see them. The roaring of the tide, and the subdued wail of the dogs, made me fear for the worst. I had to walk through the broken ice, which rose in toppling spires over my head, for nearly fifty yards, before I found an opening to the ice-face, by which I was able to climb down to them. A few cuts of a sheath-knife released them, although the caresses of the dear brutes had like to have been fatal to me, for I had to straddle with one foot on the fast ice and the other on loose piled rubbish. But I got a line attached to the cross-pieces of the sledge-runners, flung it up on the ice-foot, and then piloted my dogs out of their slough. In about ten minutes we were sweating along at eight miles an hour."

Everything looked promising, and we were only waiting for intelligence that our advance party had deposited its provisions in safety to begin our transit of the bay. Except a few sledge-lashings and some trifling accoutrements to finish, all was ready.

We were at work cheerfully, sewing away at the skins of some moccasins by the blaze of our lamps, when, toward midnight, we heard the noise of steps above, and the next minute Sontag, Ohlsen, and Petersen, came down into the cabin. Their manner startled me even more than their unexpected appearance on board. They were swollen and haggard, and hardly able to speak.

Their story was a fearful one. They had left their

companions in the ice, risking their own lives to bring us the news; Brooks, Baker, Wilson, and Pierre, were all lying frozen and disabled. Where? They could not tell; somewhere in among the hummocks to the north and east; it was drifting heavily round them when they parted. Irish Tom had stayed by to feed and care for the others; but the chances were sorely against them. It was in vain to question them further. They had evidently travelled a great distance, for they were sinking with fatigue and hunger, and could hardly be rallied enough to tell us the direction in which they had come.

My first impulse was to move on the instant with an unencumbered party; a rescue, to be effective or even hopeful, could not be too prompt. What pressed on my mind most was where the sufferers were to be looked for among the drifts. Ohlsen seemed to have his faculties rather more at command than his associates, and I thought that he might assist us as a guide; but he was sinking with exhaustion, and if he went with us we must carry him.

There was not a moment to be lost. While some were still busy with the new-comers and getting ready a hasty meal, others were rigging out the *Little Willie* with a buffalo-cover, a small tent, and a package of pemmican; and, as soon as we could hurry through our arrangements, Ohlsen was strapped on in a fur bag, his legs wrapped in dog-skins and eider down, and we were off upon the ice. Our party consisted of nine men and myself. We carried only the clothes on our backs. The thermometer stood at 46°, seventy-eight below the freezing point.

A well-known peculiar tower of ice, called by the men the "Pinnacly Berg," served as our first landmark: other icebergs of colossal size, which stretched in long faded lines across the bay, helped to guide us afterward; and it was not until we had travelled for sixteen hours that we began to lose our way.

We knew that our lost companions must be somewhere in the sea before us, within a radius of forty miles. Ohlsen, who had been for fifty hours without rest, fell asleep as soon as we began to move, and awoke now with unequivocal signs of mental disturbance. It became evident that he had lost the bearing of the icebergs, which in form and colour endlessly repeated themselves; and the uniformity of the vast field of snow utterly forbade the hope of local landmarks.

Pushing ahead of the party, and clambering over some rugged ice-piles, I came to a long level floe, which I thought might probably have attracted the eyes of weary men in circumstances like our own. It was a light conjecture; but it was enough to turn the scale, for there was no other to balance it. I gave orders to abandon the sledge, and disperse in search of footmarks. We raised our tent, placed our pemmican in *cache*, except a small allowance for each man to carry on his person; and poor Ohlsen, now just able to keep his legs, was liberated from his bag.

It was indispensable that we should move on, looking out for traces as we went. Yet when the men were ordered to spread themselves, so as to multiply the chances, though they all obeyed heartily, some painful impress of solitary danger, or perhaps it may have been the varying configuration of the ice-field, kept them closing up continually into a single group. The strange manner in which some of us were affected I now attribute as much to shattered nerves as to the direct influence of the cold. Men like M'Gary and Bonsall, who had stood out our severest marches, were seized with trembling fits and short breath; and, in spite of all my efforts to keep up an example of sound bearing, I fainted twice on the snow.

We had been nearly eighteen hours out, without water or food, when a new hope cheered us. I think it was Hans, our Esquimaux hunter, who thought he saw a broad sledge-track. The drift had nearly effaced it, and we were some of us doubtful at first whether it was not one of those accidental rifts which the gales make in the surface-snow. But, as we traced it on to the deep snow among the hummocks, we were led to footsteps; and, following these with religious care, we at last came in sight of a small American flag fluttering from a hummock, and lower down a little masonic banner hanging from a tent-pole hardly above the drift. It was the camp of our disabled comrades; we reached it after an unbroken march of twenty-one hours.

The little tent was nearly covered. I was not among the first to come up; but, when I reached the tent-curtain, the men were standing in silent file on each side of it. With more kindness and delicacy of feeling than is often supposed to belong to sailors, but which is almost characteristic, they intimated their wish that I should go in alone. As I crawled in, and, coming upon the darkness, heard before me the burst of welcome gladness that came from the four poor fellows stretched on their backs, and then for the first time the cheer outside, my weakness and my gratitude together almost overcame me. "They had expected me: they were sure I would come!"

We were now fifteen souls; the thermometer 75° below the freezing point; and our sole accommodation a tent barely able to contain eight persons: more than half our party were obliged to keep from freezing by walking outside while the others slept. We could not halt long.

Each of us took a turn of two hours' sleep, and we prepared for our homeward march.

We took with us nothing but the tent, furs to protect the rescued party, and food for a journey of fifty hours. Everything else was abandoned. Two large buffalo-bags, each made of four skins, were doubled up, so as to form a sort of sack, lined on each side by fur, closed at the bottom, but opened at the top. This was laid on the sledge; the tent, smoothly folded, serving as a floor. The sick, with their limbs sewed up carefully in reindeer-skins, were placed upon the bed of buffalo-robes, in a half-reclining posture; other skins and blanket-bags were thrown above them; and the whole litter was lashed together so as to allow but a single opening opposite the mouth for breathing.

This necessary work cost us a great deal of time and effort; but it was essential to the lives of the sufferers. It took us no less than four hours to strip and refresh them, and then to embale them in the manner I have described. Few of us escaped without frost-bitten fingers.

It was completed at last, however; all hands stood round, and after repeating a short prayer, we set out on our retreat. It was fortunate indeed that we were not inexperienced in sledging over the ice. A great part of our track lay among a succession of hummocks, some of them extending in long lines, fifteen or twenty feet high, and so uniformly steep that we had to turn them by a considerable deviation from our direct course; others that we forced our way through, far above our heads in height, lying in parallel ridges, with the space between too narrow for the sledge to be lowered into it safely, and yet not wide enough for the runners to cross without the aid of ropes to stay them. These spaces, too, were generally choked with light snow, hiding the openings between the ice-fragments. They were fearful traps to disengage a limb from, for every man knew that a fracture, or a sprain even, would cost him his life. Besides all this, the sledge was top-heavy with its load: the maimed men could not bear to be lashed down tight enough to secure them against falling off. Notwithstanding our caution in rejecting every superfluous burden, the weight, including bags and tent, was eleven hundred pounds.

And yet our march for the first six hours was very cheering. We made, by vigorous pulls and lifts, nearly a mile an hour, and reached the new floes before we were absolutely weary. Our sledge sustained the trial admirably. Ohlsen, restored by hope, walked steadily at the leading belt of the sledge lines; and I began to feel certain of reaching our half-way station of the day before, where we had left our tent. But we were still nine miles from it, when, almost without premonition, we all became aware of an alarming failure of our energies.

Bonsall and Morton, two of our stoutest men, came to me, begging permission to sleep. "They were not cold, the wind did not enter them now,—a little sleep was all they wanted." Presently Hans was found nearly stiff under a drift; and Thomas, bolt upright, had his eyes closed, and could hardly articulate. At last John Blake threw himself on the snow, and refused to rise. They did not complain of feeling cold; but it was in vain that I wrestled, boxed, ran, argued, jeered, or reprimanded: an immediate halt could not be avoided.

We pitched our tent with much difficulty. Our hands were too powerless to strike a fire; we were obliged to do without water or food. Even the spirits (whisky) had frozen at the men's feet, under all the coverings. We put Bonsall, Ohlsen, Thomas, and Hans, with the other sick men, well inside the tent, and crowded in as many others as we could. Then, leaving the party in charge of Mr M'Gary, with orders to come on after four hours' rest, I pushed ahead with William Godfrey, who volunteered to be my companion. My aim was to reach the half-way tent, and thaw some ice and pemmican before the others arrived.

The floe was of level ice, and the walking excellent. I cannot tell how long it took us to make the nine miles, for we were in a strange sort of stupor, and had little apprehension of time. It was probably about four hours. We kept ourselves awake by imposing on each other a continued articulation of words; they must have been incoherent enough. I recall these hours as among the most wretched I have ever gone through: we were neither of us in our right senses, and retained a very confused recollection of what preceded our arrival at the tent. We both of us, however, remember a bear, who walked leisurely before us, and tore up as he went a jumper that Mr M'Gary had improvidently thrown off the day before. He tore it into shreds and rolled it into a ball, but never offered to interfere with our progress. I remember this, and with it a confused sentiment that our tent and buffalo-robes might probably share the same fate. Godfrey, with whom the memory of this day's work may atone for many faults of a later time, had a better eye than myself; and, looking some miles ahead, he could see that our tent was undergoing the same unceremonious treatment. I thought I saw it too, but we were so drunken with cold that we strode on steadily, and, for aught I know, without quickening our pace.

Probably our approach saved the contents of the tent; for when we reached it the tent was uninjured, though the bear had overturned it, tossing the buffalo-robes and pemmican into the snow; we missed only a couple of blanket-bags. What we recollect, however,—and perhaps all we recollect,—is, that we had great difficulty in raising it. We crawled into our reindeer sleeping-bags without speaking, and for the next three hours slept on in a dreamy but intense slumber. When I awoke, my long beard was a mass of ice, frozen fast to the buffalo-skin; Godfrey had to cut me out with his jack-knife. Four days after our escape, I found my woollen comfortable with a goodly share of my beard still adhering to it.

We were able to melt water and get some soup cooked before the rest of our party arrived: it took them but five hours to walk the nine miles. They were doing well, and, considering the circumstances, in wonderful spirits. The day was almost providentially windless, with a clear sun. All enjoyed the refreshment we had got ready: the crippled were repacked in their robes; and we sped briskly toward the hummock-ridges which lay between us and the Pinnacly Berg.

It required desperate efforts to work our way over it—literally desperate, for our strength failed us anew, and we began to lose our self-control. We could not abstain any longer from eating snow; our mouths swelled, and some of us became speechless.

Our halts multiplied, and we fell half-sleeping on the snow. I could not prevent it. Strange to say, it refreshed us. I ventured upon the experiment myself, making Riley wake me at the end of three minutes; and I felt so much benefited by it that I timed the men in the same way. They sat on the runners of the sledge, fell asleep instantly, and were forced to wakefulness when their three minutes were out.

By eight in the evening we emerged from the floes. The sight of Pinnacly Berg revived us. Brandy, an invaluable resource in emergency, had already been served out in table-spoonful doses. We now took a longer rest, and a last but stouter dram, and reached the brig at 1 P.M., we believe without a halt.

I say *we believe;* and here perhaps is the most decided proof of our sufferings; we were quite delirious, and had ceased to entertain a sane apprehension of the circumstances about us. We moved on like men in a dream. Our footmarks seen afterward showed that we had steered a straight line for the brig. It must have been by a sort of instinct, for it left no impress on the memory. Bonsall was sent staggering ahead, and reached the brig, God knows how, for he had fallen repeatedly at the track-lines; but he delivered with punctilious accuracy the messages I had sent by him to Dr Hayes. I thought myself the soundest of all, for I went through all the formula of sanity, and can recall the muttering delirium of my comrades when we got back into the cabin of our brig. Yet I have been told since of some speeches and some orders too of mine, which I should have remembered for their absurdity, if my mind had retained its balance.

Petersen and Whipple came out to meet us about two miles from the brig. They brought my dog-team, with the restoratives I had sent for by Bonsall. I do not remember their coming. Dr Hayes entered with judicious energy upon the treatment our condition called for, administering morphine freely, after the usual frictions. He reported none of our brain-symptoms as serious, referring them properly to the class of those indications of exhausted power which yield to generous diet and rest. Mr Ohlsen suffered some time from strabismus and blindness; two others underwent amputation of parts of the foot without unpleasant consequences, and two died in spite of all our efforts. This rescue-party had been out for seventy-two hours. We had halted in all eight hours, half of our number sleeping at a time. We travelled between eighty and ninety miles, most of the way dragging a heavy sledge. The mean temperature of the whole time, including the warmest hours of three days, was at — 41°·2. We had no water except at our halts, and were at no time able to intermit vigorous exercise without freezing.

"*April* 4.—Four days have passed, and I am again at my record of failures, sound, but aching still in every joint. The rescued men are not out of danger, but their gratitude is very touching. Pray God that they may live!"

CHAPTER VII.

THE FIRST STRANGE FACES—THE ESQUIMAUX.

THE week that followed has left me nothing to remember but anxieties and sorrow. Nearly all our party, as well the rescuers as the rescued, were tossing in their sick-bunks, some frozen, others undergoing amputations, several with dreadful premonitions of tetanus. I was myself among the first to be about; the necessities of the others claimed it of me.

Early in the morning of the 7th I was awakened by a sound from Baker's throat, one of those the most frightful and ominous that ever startle a physician's ear. The lockjaw had seized him—that dark visitant whose foreshadowings were on so many of us. His symptoms marched rapidly to their result; he died the next day. On the 9th we placed him in his coffin, and, forming a rude, but heartfull procession, bore him over the broken ice and up the steep side of the ice-foot to Butler Island; then, passing along the snow-level to Fern Rock, and climbing the slope of the Observatory, we deposited his corpse upon the pedestals which had served to support our instruments. We read the service for the burial of the dead, sprinkling over him snow for dust, and repeated the Lord's Prayer; and then icing up again the opening in the walls we had made to admit the coffin, left him in his narrow house.

We were watching in the morning at Baker's death-bed, when one of our deck-watch, who had been cutting ice for the melter, came hurrying down into the cabin with the report, "People holloaing ashore!" I went up, followed by as many as could mount the gangway; and there they were, on all sides of our rocky harbour, dotting the snow-shores and emerging from the blackness of the cliffs,—wild and uncouth, but evidently human beings.

As we gathered on the deck, they rose upon the more elevated fragments of the land-ice, and distributing themselves around almost in a half-circle. They were vociferating as if to attract our attention, or perhaps only to give vent to their surprise; but I could make nothing out of their cries, except "Hoah, ha, ha!" and "Ka, kääh! ka, kääh!" repeated over and over again.

There was light enough for me to see that they brandished no weapons, and were only tossing their heads and arms about in violent gesticulations. A more unexcited inspection showed us, too, that their numbers were not as great· nor their size as large as some of us had been disposed to fancy at first. In a word, I was satisfied that they were natives of the country; and, calling Petersen from his bunk to be my interpreter, I proceeded unarmed, and waving my open hands, toward a stout figure who made himself conspicuous, and seemed to have a greater number near him than the rest. He evidently understood the movement, for he at once, like a brave fellow, leaped down upon the floe and advanced to meet me fully half-way.

He was nearly a head taller than myself, extremely powerful and well-built, with swarthy complexion and piercing black eyes. His dress was a hooded *capôte* or jumper of mixed white and blue fox-pelts, arranged with something of fancy, and booted trousers of white bear-skin, which at the end of the foot were made to terminate with the claws of the animal.

I soon came to an understanding with this gallant diplomatist. Almost as soon as we commenced our parley, his companions, probably receiving signals from him, flocked in and surrounded us; but we had no difficulty in making them know positively that they must remain where they were, while Metek went with me on board the ship. This gave me the advantage of negotiating with an important hostage.

Although this was the first time he had ever seen a white man, he went with me fearlessly; his companions staying behind on the ice. Hickey took them out what he esteemed our greatest delicacies,—slices of good wheat bread and corned pork, with exorbitant lumps of white sugar; but they refused to touch them. They had evidently no apprehension of open violence from us. I found afterward that several among them were singly a match for the white bear and the walrus, and that they thought us a very pale-faced crew.

OUTFIT OF THE ESQUIMAUX.

Being satisfied with my interview in the cabin, I sent out word that the rest might be admitted to the ship; and, although they, of course, could not know how their chief had been dealt with, some nine or ten of them followed with boisterous readiness upon the bidding. Others in the meantime, as if disposed to give us their company for the full time of a visit, brought up from behind the land-ice as many as fifty-six fine dogs, with their sledges, and secured them within two hundred feet of the brig, driving their lances into the ice, and picketing the dogs to them by the seal-skin traces. The animals understood the operation perfectly, and lay down as soon as it commenced. The sledges were made up of small fragments of porous bone, admirably knit together by thongs of hide; the runners, which glistened like burnished steel, were of highly-polished ivory, obtained from the tusks of the walrus.

The only arms they carried were knives, concealed in their boots; but their lances, which were lashed to the sledges, were quite a formidable weapon. The staff was of the horn of the narwhal, or else of the thigh-bones of the bear, two lashed together, or sometimes the mirabilis of the walrus, three or four of them united. This last was a favourite material also for the cross-bars of their sledges. They had no wood. A single rusty hoop from a current-drifted cask might have furnished all the knives of the party; but the fleam-shaped tips of their lances were of unmistakable steel, and were rivetted to the tapering bony point with no mean skill. I learned afterward that the metal was obtained in traffic from the more southern tribes.

They were clad much as I have described Metek, in jumpers, boots, and white bear-skin breeches, with their feet decorated like his, *en griffe*. A strip of knotted leather worn round the neck, very greasy and dirty-looking, which no one could be persuaded to part with for an instant, was mistaken at first for an ornament by the crew: it was not until mutual hardships had made us better acquainted that we learned its mysterious uses.

When they were first allowed to come on board, they were very rude and difficult to manage. They spoke three or four at a time, to each other and to us, laughing heartily at our ignorance in not understanding them, and then talking away as before. They were incessantly in motion, going everywhere, trying doors, and squeezing themselves through dark passages, round casks and boxes, and out into the light again, anxious to touch and handle everything they saw, and asking for, or else endeavouring to steal, everything they touched. It was the more difficult to restrain them, as I did not wish them to suppose that we were at all intimidated. But there were some signs of our disabled condition which it was important they should not see; it was especially necessary to keep them out of the forecastle, where the dead body of poor Baker was lying; and, as it was in vain to reason or persuade, we had at last to employ the "gentle laying-on of hands," which, I believe, the laws of all countries tolerate, to keep them in order.

Our whole force was mustered and kept constantly on the alert; but though there may have been something of discourtesy in the occasional shoulderings and hustlings that enforced the police of the ship, things went on good-humouredly. Our guests continued running in and out and about the vessel, bringing in provisions, and carrying them out again to their dogs on the ice,—in fact, stealing all the time until the afternoon, when, like tired children, they threw themselves down to sleep. I ordered them to be made comfortable in the hold; and Morton spread a large buffalo-robe for them, not far from a coal-fire in the galley-stove.

They were lost in barbarous amaze at the new fuel,—too hard for blubber, too soft for firestone,—but they were content to believe it might cook as well as seals' fat. They borrowed from us an iron pot and some melted water, and parboiled a couple of pieces of walrus-meat; but the real *pièce de resistance*, some five pounds a head, they preferred to eat raw. Yet there was something of the *gourmet* in their mode of assorting their mouthfuls of beef and blubber Slices of each, or rather strips, passed between the lips, either together or in strict alternation, and with a regularity of sequence that kept the molars well to their work.

They did not eat all at once, but each man when and as often as the impulse prompted. Each slept after eating, his raw meat lying beside him on the buffalo-skin; and as he woke, the first act was to eat, and the next to sleep again. They did not lie down, but slumbered away in a sitting posture, with the head declined upon the breast, some of them snoring famously.

In the morning they were anxious to go; but I had given orders to detain them for a parting interview with myself. It resulted in a treaty, brief in its terms, that it might be certainly remembered, and mutually beneficial, that it might possibly be kept. I tried to make them understand what a powerful Prospero they had had for a host, and how beneficent he would prove himself so long as they did his bidding. And, as an earnest of my favour, I bought all the walrus-meat they had to spare, and four of their dogs, enriching them in return with needles and beads, and a treasure of old cask-staves.

In the fulness of their gratitude, they pledged themselves emphatically to return in a few days with more meat, and to allow me to use their dogs and sledges for my excursions to the north. I then gave them leave to go. They yoked in their dogs in less than two minutes, got on their sledges, cracked their two-fathom-and-a-half-long sealskin whips, and were off down the ice to the south-west at a rate of seven knots an hour.

They did not return. I had read enough of treaty-makings not to expect them too confidently. But the next day came a party of five, on foot—two old men, one of middle age, and a couple of gawky boys. We had missed a number of articles soon after the first party left us, an axe, a saw, and some knives. We found afterward that our storehouse at Butler Island had been entered; we were too short-handed to guard it by a special watch. Besides all this, reconnoitring stealthily beyond Sylvia Head, we discovered a train of sledges drawn up behind the hummocks.

There was cause for apprehension in all this; but I felt that I could not afford to break with the rogues. They had it in their power to molest us seriously in our sledge-travel; they could make our hunts around the harbour dangerous; and my best chance of obtaining an abundant supply of fresh meat, our great desideratum, was by their agency. I treated the new party with marked kindness, and gave them many presents; but took care to make them aware that, until all the missing articles were restored, no member of the tribe would be admitted again as a guest on board the brig. They went off with many pantomimic protestations of innocence; but M'Gary, nevertheless, caught the incorrigible scamps stealing a coal-barrel as they passed Butler Island, and expedited their journey homeward by firing among them a charge of small shot.

Still, one peculiar worthy—we thought it must have been the venerable of the party, whom I knew afterwards as a staunch friend, old Shang-huh—managed to work round in a westerly direction, and to cut to pieces my India-rubber boat, which had been left on the floe since Mr Brook's disaster, and to carry off every particle of the wood.

A few days after this, an agile, elfin youth drove up to our floe in open day. He was sprightly and good-looking, and had quite a neat turn-out of sledge and dogs. He told his name with frankness,—"*Myouk*, I am,"—and where he lived. We asked him about the boat; but he denied all knowledge of it, and refused either to confess or repent. He was surprised when I ordered him to be confined to the hold. At first he refused to eat, and sat down in the deepest grief; but after a while he began to sing, and then to talk and cry, and then to sing again; and he kept crying, singing, and talking by turns, till a late hour of the night. When I turned in, he was still noisily disconsolate.

There was a simplicity and *bonhommie* about this boy that interested me much; and I confess that when I made my appearance next morning—I could hardly conceal it from the gentleman on duty, whom I affected to censure—I was glad my bird had flown. Some time during the morning-watch he had succeeded in throwing off the hatch and escaping. We suspected that he had confederates ashore, for his dogs had escaped with as much address as himself. I was convinced, however, that I had the truth from him, where he lived, and how many lived with him —my cross-examination on these points having been very complete and satisfactory.

It was a sad business for some time after these Esquimaux left us, to go on making and registering our observations at Fern Rock. Baker's corpse still lay in the vestibule, and it was not long before another was placed by the side of it. We had to pass the bodies as often as we went in or out; but the men, grown feeble and nervous, disliked going near them in the night-time. When the summer thaw came, and we could gather stones enough, we built up a grave on a depression of the rocks, and raised a substantial cairn above it.

"*April* 19.—I have been out on the floe again, breaking in my dogs. My reinforcement from the Esquimaux makes a noble team for me. For the last five days I have been striving with them, just as often and as long as my strength allowed me; and to-day I have my victory. The Society for Preventing Cruelty to Animals would have put me in custody if they had been near enough; but, thanks to a merciless whip freely administered, I have been dashing along twelve miles in the last hour, and am back again; harness, sledge, and bones all unbroken. I am ready for another journey.

"*April* 22.—Schubert has increasing symptoms of erysipelas around his amputated stump; and every one on board is depressed and silent except himself. He is singing in his bunk, as joyously as ever. Poor fellow! I am alarmed about him: it is a hard duty which compels me to take the field, while my presence might cheer his last moments."

CHAPTER VIII.

A NEW EXPLORATION—RETURN OF SPRING.

The month of April was about to close, and the short season available for Arctic search was upon us. The condition of things on board the brig was not such as I could have wished for; but there was nothing to exact my presence, and it seemed to me clear that the time had come for pressing on the work of the expedition. The arrangements for our renewed exploration had not been intermitted, and were soon complete. I leave to my journal its own story.

"*April 25.*—A journey on the carpet, and the crew busy with the little details of their outfit: the officers the same.

"*April 26.*—These Esquimaux must be watched carefully; at the same time they are to be dealt with kindly, though with a strict enforcement of our police regulations, and some caution as to the freedom with which they may come on board. No punishments must be permitted, either of them or in their presence, and no resort to fire-arms unless to repel a serious attack. I have given orders, however, that if the contingency does occur, there shall be no firing over head. The *prestige* of the gun with a savage is in his notion of its infallibility. You may spare bloodshed by killing a dog, or even wounding him; but in no event should you throw away your ball. It is neither politic nor humane.

"Our stowage precautions are all arranged, to meet the chance of the ice breaking up while I am away; and a boat is placed ashore with stores, as the brig may be forced from her moorings.

"The worst thought I have now in setting out is, that of the entire crew I can leave but two behind in able condition, and the doctor and Bonsall are the only two officers who can help Ohlsen. This is our force, four able-bodied, and six disabled, to keep the brig; the commander and seven men, scarcely better upon the average, out upon the ice. Eighteen souls, thank God! certainly not eighteen bodies!

"I am going this time to follow the ice-belt to the Great Glacier of Humboldt, and there load up with pemmican from our *cache* of last October. From this point I expect to stretch along the face of the glacier inclining to the west of north, and make an attempt to cross the ice to the American side. Once on smooth ice, near this shore, I may pass to the west, and enter the large indentation whose existence I can infer with nearly positive certainty. In this I may find an outlet, and determine the state of things beyond the ice-clogged area of this bay.

"I take with me pemmican, bread, and tea, a canvas tent, five feet by six, and two sleeping bags of reindeer-skin. The sledge has been built on board by Mr Ohlsen. It is very light, of hickory, and but nine feet long. Our kitchen is a soup-kettle for melting snow and making tea, arranged so as to boil with either lard or spirits.

"M'Gary has taken the *Faith*. He carries few stores, intending to replenish at the *cache* of Bonsall Point, and to lay in pemmican at M'Gary Island. Most of his cargo consists of bread, which we find it hard to dispense with in eating cooked food. It has a good effect in absorbing the fat of the pemmican, which is apt to disagree with the stomach."

Godfrey and myself followed on the 27th, as I had intended. The journey was an arduous one to be undertaken, even under the most favouring circumstances, and by unbroken men. It was to be the crowning expedition of the campaign, to attain the *Ultima Thule* of the Greenland shore, measure the waste that lay between it and the unknown West, and seek round the furthest circle of the ice for an outlet to the mysterious channels beyond. The scheme could not be carried out in its details; yet it was prosecuted far enough to indicate what must be our future fields of labour, and to determine many points of geographical interest. Our observations were in general confirmatory of those which had been made by Mr Bonsall; and they accorded so well with our subsequent surveys as to trace for us the outline of the coast with great certainty.

"It is now the 20th of May, and for the first time I am able, propped up by pillows and surrounded by sick messmates, to note the fact that we have failed again to force the passage to the north.

"Godfrey and myself overtook the advance party under M'Gary two days after leaving the brig. Our dogs were in fair travelling condition, and, except snow-blindness, there seemed to be no drawback to our efficiency. In crossing Marshall Bay we found the snow so accumulated in drifts that, with all our efforts to pick out a track, we became involved; we could not force our sledges through. We were forced to unload, and carry forward the cargo on our backs, beating a path for the dogs to follow in. In this way we plodded on to the opposite headland, Cape William Wood, where the waters of Mary Minturn River, which had delayed the freezing of the ice, gave us a long reach of level travel. We then made a better rate; and our days' marches were such as to carry us by the 4th of May nearly to the glacier.

"This progress, however, was dearly earned. As early as the 3d of May the winter's scurvy re-appeared painfully among our party. As we struggled through the snow along the Greenland coast we sank up to our middle; and the dogs, floundering about, were so buried as to preclude any attempts at hauling. Here three of the party were taken with snow-blindness, and George Stephenson had to be condemned as unfit for travel altogether, on account of chest-symptoms accompanying his scorbutic troubles. On the 4th Thomas Hickey also gave in, although not quite disabled for labour at the track-lines.

"Perhaps we would still have got on; but, to crown all, we found that the bears had effected an entrance into our pemmican casks, and destroyed our chances of reinforcing our provisions at the several *caches*. This great calamity was certainly inevitable; for it is simple justice to the officers under whose charge the provision depôts were constructed, to say that no means in their power could have prevented the result. The pemmican was covered with blocks of stone, which it had required the labour of three men to adjust; but the extraordinary strength of the bear had enabled him to force aside the heaviest rocks, and his pawing had broken the iron casks which held our pemmican literally into chips. Our alcohol cask, which it had cost me a separate and special journey in the late fall to deposit, was so completely destroyed that we could not find a stave of it.

"Off Cape James Kent, about eight miles from 'Sunny Gorge,' while taking an observation for latitude, I was myself seized with a sudden pain, and fainted. My limbs became rigid, and certain obscure tetanoid symptoms of our late winter's enemy disclosed themselves. In this condition I was unable to make more than nine miles a day. I was strapped upon the sledge, and the march continued as usual; but my powers diminished so rapidly that I could not resist even the otherwise comfortable temperament of 5° below zero. My left foot becoming frozen, caused a vexatious delay; and the same night it became evident that the immovability of my limbs was due to dropsical effusion.

"On the 5th, becoming delirious, and fainting every time that I was taken from the tent to the sledge, I succumbed entirely.

"The scurvy had already broken out among the men, with symptoms like my own; and Morton, our strongest man, was beginning to give way. It is the reverse of comfort to me that they shared my weakness. All that I should remember with pleasurable feeling is, that to five brave men,—Morton, Riley, Hickey, Stephenson, and Hans, themselves scarcely able to travel,—I owe my preservation. They carried me back by forced marches, and I was taken into the brig on the 14th. Since then, fluctuating between life and death, I have by the blessing of God reached the present date, and see feebly in prospect my recovery. Dr Hayes regards my attack as one of scurvy, complicated by typhoid fever. George Stephenson is similarly affected. Our worst symptoms are dropsical effusion and night-sweats.

"*May* 22.—Let me, if I can, make up my record for the time I have been away, or on my back.

"Poor Schubert is gone. Our gallant, merry-hearted companion left us some ten days ago, for, I trust, a more genial world. It is sad, in this dreary little homestead of ours, to miss his contented face and the joyous troll of his ballads.

"The health of the rest has, if anything, improved. Their complexions show the influence of sunlight, and I think several have a firmer and more elastic step. Stephenson and Thomas are the only two beside myself who are likely to suffer permanently from the effects of our breakdown. Bad scurvy both: symptoms still serious.

"I left Hans as hunter. I gave him a regular exemption from all other labour, and a promised present to his lady-love on reaching Fiskernaes. He signalised his promotion by shooting two deer, *Tukkuk*, the first yet shot. We have now on hand one hundred and forty-five pounds of venison, a very gift of grace to our diseased crew. But, indeed, we are not likely to want for wholesome food, now that the night is gone, which made our need of it so pressing. On the first of May those charming little migrants, the snow-birds, *ultima cœlicolum*, which only left us on the 4th of November, returned to our ice-crusted rocks, whence they seem to 'fill the sea and air with their sweet jargoning.' Seal literally abound, too. I have learned to prefer this flesh to the reindeer's, at least that of the female seal, which has not the fetor of her mate's.

"By the 12th, the sides of the *Advance* were free from snow, and her rigging clean and dry. The floe is rapidly undergoing its wonderful processes of decay, and the level ice measures but six feet in thickness. To-day they report a burgomaster-gull seen, one of the earliest but surest indications of returning open water. It is not strange, ice-leaguered exiles as we are, that we observe and exult in these things. They are the pledges of renewed life, the olive-branch of this dreary waste: we feel the spring in all our pulses.

"The first thing I did after my return was to send M'Gary to the Life-boat Cove, to see that our boat and its buried provisions were secure. He made the journey by dog-sledge in four days, and has returned reporting that all is safe—an important help for us, should this heavy ice of our more northern prison refuse to release us.

"But the pleasantest feature of his journey was the disclosure of open water, extending up in a sort of tongue, with a trend of north by east to within two miles of Refuge Harbour, and there widening as it expanded to the south and west.

"As soon as I had recovered enough to be aware of my failure, I began to devise means for remedying it. But I found the resources of the party shattered. Pierre had died but a week before, and his death exerted an unfavourable influence. There were only three men able to do duty. Of the officers, Wilson, Brooks, Sontag, and Petersen, were knocked up. There was no one except Sontag, Hayes, or myself who was qualified to conduct a survey; and, of us three, Dr Hayes was the only one on his feet.

"The quarter to which our remaining observations were to be directed lay to the north and east of the Cape Sabine of Captain Inglefield. The interruption our progress along the coast of Greenland had met from the Great Glacier, and destruction of our provision-caches by the bears, left a blank for us of the entire northern coast-line. It was necessary to ascertain whether the farthermost expansion of Smith's Strait did not find an outlet in still more remote channels.

"I determined to trust almost entirely to the dogs for our travel in the future, and to send our parties of exploration, one after the other, as rapidly as the strength and refreshing of our team would permit.

"Dr Hayes was selected for that purpose; and I satisfied myself that, with a little assistance from my comrades,

I could be carried round to the cots of the sick, and so avail myself of his services in the field.

"He was a perfectly fresh man, not having yet undertaken a journey. I gave him a team and my best driver, William Godfrey. He is to cross Smith's Straits above the inlet, and make as near as may be a straight course for Cape Sabine. My opinion is, that by keeping well south he will find the ice less clogged and easier sledging. Our experience proves, I think, that the transit of this broken area must be most impeded as we approach the glacier. The immense discharge of icebergs cannot fail to break it up seriously for travel.

"I gave him the small sledge which was built by Ohlsen. The snow was sufficiently thawed to make it almost unnecessary to use fire as a means of obtaining water; they could therefore dispense with tallow or alcohol, and were able to carry pemmican in larger quantities. Their sleeping-bags were a very neat article of a light reindeer-skin. The dogs were in excellent condition too—no longer foot-sore, but well rested and completely broken, including the four from the Esquimaux, animals of great power and size. Two of these, the stylish leaders of the team, a span of thoroughly wolfish iron-greys, have the most powerful and wild-beast-like bound that I have seen in animals of their kind.

"I made up the orders of the party on the 19th, the first day that I was able to mature a plan; and with commendable zeal they left the brig on the 20th.

"*May* 23.—They have had superb weather, thank heaven!—a profusion of the most genial sunshine, bringing out the seals in crowds to bask around their breathing-holes. Winter has gone!

"*May* 26.—I get little done; but I have too much to

attend to in my weak state to journalise. Thermometer above freezing-point, without the sun to-day.

"*May* 27.—Everything showing that the summer-changes have commenced. The ice is rapidly losing its integrity, and a melting snow has fallen for the last two days,—one of those comforting home-snows that we have not seen for so long.

"*May* 28.—Our day of rest and devotion. It was a fortnight ago last Friday since our poor friend Pierre died. For nearly two months he had been struggling against the enemy with a resolute will and mirthful spirit, that seemed sure of victory; but he sunk in spite of them.

"The last offices were rendered to him with the same careful ceremonial that we observed at Baker's funeral. There were fewer to walk in the procession; but the body was encased in a decent pine coffin, and carried to Observatory Island, where it was placed side by side with that of his messmate. Neither could yet be buried; but it is hardly necessary to say that the frost has embalmed their remains. Dr Hayes read the chapter from Job which has consigned so many to their last resting-place, and a little snow was sprinkled upon the face of the coffin. Pierre was a volunteer not only of our general expedition, but of the party with which he met his death-blow. He was a gallant man, a universal favourite on board, always singing some Béranger ballad or other, and so elastic in his merriment, that even in his last sickness he cheered all that were about him.

"*May* 30.—We are gleaning fresh water from the rocks, and the icebergs begin to show commencing streamlets. The great floe is no longer a Sahara, if still a desert. The floes are wet, and their snow dissolve readily under the warmth of the foot, and the old floe begins to shed fresh water into its hollows. Puddles of salt water collect around the ice-foot. It is now hardly recognisable,—rounded, sunken, broken up with water-pools overflowing its base. Its diminished crusts are so percolated by the saline tides, that neither tables nor broken fragments unite any longer by freezing. It is lessening so rapidly that we do not fear it any longer as an enemy to the brig. The berg indeed vanished long before the sun-thermometers indicated a noon temperature above 32°.

Seal grow still more numerous on the level floes, lying cautiously in the sun beside their breathing-holes. By means of the Esquimaux stratagem of a white screen pushed forward on a sledge until the concealed hunter comes within range, Hans has shot four of them. We have more fresh meat than we can eat. For the past three weeks we have been living on ptarmigan, rabbits, two reindeer, and seal.

"They are fast curing our scurvy. With all these resources, coming to our relief so suddenly too, how can my thoughts turn despairingly to poor Franklin and his crew?

"Can they have survived? No man can answer with certainty; but no man without presumption can answer in the negative.

"If, four months ago,—surrounded by darkness and bowed down by disease,—I had been asked the question, I would have turned toward the black hills and the frozen sea, and responded in sympathy with them, 'No.' But with the return of light a savage people come down upon us, destitute of any but the rudest appliances of the chase, who were fattening on the most wholesome diet of the region, only forty miles from our anchorage, while I was denouncing its scarcity."

CHAPTER IX.

ADVENT OF THE SECOND YEAR.

"*May* 30, 1854.—It is a year ago to-day since we left New York. I am not as sanguine as I was then: time and experience have chastened me. There is everything about me to check enthusiasm and moderate hope. I am here in forced inaction, a broken-down man, oppressed by cares, with many dangers before me, and still under the shadow of a hard wearing winter, which has crushed two of my best associates. Here, on the spot, after two unavailing expeditions of search, I hold my opinions unchanged; and I record them as a matter of duty upon a manuscript which may speak the truth when I can do so no longer.

"*June* 1.—At ten o'clock this morning the wail of the dogs outside announced the return of Dr Hayes and William Godfrey. Both of them were completely snow-blind, and the doctor had to be led to my bedside to make his report. In fact, so exhausted was he, that in spite of my anxiety I forbore to question him until he had rested. I venture to say, that both he and his companion well remember their astonishing performance over stewed-apples and seal-meat.

"The dogs were not so foot-sore as might have been expected; but two of them, including poor little Jenny, were completely knocked up. All attention was bestowed on these indispensable essentials of Arctic search, and soon they were more happy than their masters."

Dr Hayes had made a due north line on leaving the

brig; but, encountering the "squeezed ices" of my own party in March, he wisely worked to the eastward.

On the 22d he encountered a wall of hummocks, exceeding twenty feet in height, and extending in a long line to the north-east.

After vain attempts to force them, becoming embarrassed in fragmentary ice,—worn, to use his own words, into "deep pits and valleys,"—he was obliged to camp, surrounded by masses of the wildest character, some of them thirty feet in height.

The next three days were spent in struggles through this broken plain; fogs sometimes embarrassed them, but at intervals land could be seen to the north-west. On the 27th they reached the north side of the bay, passing over but few miles of new and unbroken floe.

Dr Hayes told me, that in many places they could not have advanced a step but for the dogs. Deep cavities filled with snow intervened between lines of ice-barricades, making their travel as slow and tedious as the same obstructions had done to the party of poor Brooks before their eventful rescue last March.

His journal entry, referring to the 23d, while tangled in the ice, says, "I was so snow-blind that I could not see; and as riding, owing to the jaded condition of the dogs, was seldom possible, we were obliged to lay-to."

It was not until the 25th that their eyesight was sufficiently restored to enable them to push on. In these devious and untrodden ice-fields, even the instinct of the dogs would have been of little avail to direct their course. It was well for the party that during this compulsory halt the temperatures were mild and endurable.

On the 26th, disasters accumulated. William Godfrey, one of the sturdiest travellers, broke down; and the dogs, the indispensable reliance of the party, were in bad working trim. The rude harness, always apt to become tangled and broken, had been mended so often, and with such imperfect means, as to be scarcely serviceable.

This evil would seem the annoyance of an hour to the travellers in a stage-coach, but to a sledge-party on the ice-waste it is the gravest that can be conceived. The Esquimaux dog is driven by a single trace, a long thin thong of seal or walrus hide, which passes from his chest over his haunches to the sledge. The team is always driven abreast, and the traces are of course tangling and twisting themselves up incessantly, as the half-wild or terrified brutes bound right or left from their prescribed positions. The consequence is, that the seven or nine or fourteen lines have a marvellous aptitude at knotting themselves up beyond the reach of skill and patience. If the weather is warm enough to thaw the snow, they become utterly soft and flaccid, and the naked hand, if applied ingeniously, may dispense with a resort to the Gordian process; but in the severe cold, such as I experienced in my winter journeys of 1854, the knife is often the only appliance,— an unsafe one if invoked too often, for every new attachment shortens your harness, and you may end by drawing your dogs so close that they cannot pull. I have been obliged to halt and camp on the open floe, till I could renew enough of warmth and energy and patience to disentangle the knots of my harness.

It was only after appropriating an undue share of his seal-skin breeches that the leader of the party succeeded in patching up his mutilated dog-lines. He was rewarded, however, for he shortly after found an old floe, over which his sledge passed happily to the north coast. It was the first time that any of our parties had succeeded in penetrating the area to the north. The ice had baffled three organized foot-parties. It would certainly never have been traversed without the aid of dogs; but it is equally certain that the effort must again have failed, even with their aid, but for the energy and determination of Dr Hayes, and the endurance of his partner, William Godfrey.

The party spent the 28th in mending the sledge, which was completely broken, and feeding up their dogs for a renewal of the journey. But, their provisions being limited, Dr Hayes did not deem himself justified in continuing to the north. He determined to follow and survey the coast toward Cape Sabine.

His pemmican was reduced to eighteen pounds; there was apparently no hope of deriving resources from the hunt; and the coasts were even more covered with snow than those he had left on the southern side. His return was a thing of necessity.

Most providentially they found the passage home free from bergs; but their provisions were nearly gone, and their dogs were exhausted. They threw away their sleeping-bags, which were of reindeer-skin and weighed about twelve pounds each, and abandoned, besides, clothing enough to make up a reduction in weight of nearly fifty pounds. With their load so lightened, they were enabled to make good the crossing of the bay. They landed at Peter Force Bay, and reached the brig on the 1st of June.

This journey connected the northern coast with the former surveys; but it disclosed no channel or any form of exit from this bay.

It convinced me, however, that such a channel must exist; for this great curve could be no *cul-de-sac*. Even were my observations since my first fall-journey of September 1853, not decisive on this head, the general movement of the icebergs, the character of the tides, and the equally sure analogies of physical geography, would point unmistakably to such a conclusion.

To verify it, I at once commenced the organization of a double party. This, which is called in my Report the North-east Party, was to be assisted by dogs, but was to be subsisted as far as the Great Glacier by provisions carried by a foot-party in advance.

For the continuation of my plans I again refer to my journal.

"*June* 2.—There is still this hundred miles wanting to the north-west to complete our entire circuit of this frozen water. This is to be the field for our next party. I am at some loss how to organize it. For myself, I am down with scurvy. Dr Hayes is just from the field, worn-out and snow-blind, and the health-roll of the crew makes a sorry parade.

"*June* 3.—M'Gary, Bonsall, Hickey, and Riley were detailed for the first section of the new parties; they will be accompanied by Morton, who has orders to keep himself as fresh as possible, so as to enter on his own line of search to the greatest possible advantage. I keep Hans a while to recruit the dogs, and do the hunting and locomotion generally for the rest of us; but I shall soon let him follow, unless things grow so much worse on board as to make it impossible.

"I am intensely anxious that this party should succeed; it is my last throw. They have all my views, and I believe they will carry them out unless overruled by a higher power.

"Their orders are, to carry the sledge forward as far as the base of the Great Glacier, and fill up their provisions from the *cache* of my own party of last May. Hans will then join them with the dogs; and, while M'Gary and three men attempt to scale and survey the glacier, Morton and Hans will push to the north across the bay with the dog-sledge, and advance along the more distant coast. Both divisions are provided with clampers, to steady them and their sledges on the irregular ice-surfaces; but I am not without apprehensions that, with all their efforts, the glacier cannot be surmounted.

"In this event, the main reliance must be on Mr Morton. He takes with him a sextant, artificial horizon, and pocket chronometer, and has intelligence, courage, and the spirit of endurance in full measure. He is withal a long-tried and trustworthy follower.

"*June* 5.—The last party are off; they left yesterday at 2 P.M. I can do nothing more but await the ice-changes that are to determine for us our liberation or continued imprisonment.

"*June* 6.—We are a parcel of sick men, affecting to keep ship till our comrades get back. Except Mr Ohlsen and George Whipple, there is not a sound man among us. Thus wearily in our Castle of Indolence, for 'labour dire it was, and weary woe,' we have been watching the changing days, and noting bird, insect, and vegetable, as it tells us of the coming summer. One fly buzzed around William Godfrey's head to-day,—he could not tell what the species was; and Mr Petersen brought in a cocoon from which the grub had eaten its way to liberty. Hans gives us a seal almost daily, and for a passing luxury we have ptarmigan and hare. The little snow-birds have crowded to Butler Island, and their songs penetrate the cracks of our rude housing. Another snipe, too, was mercilessly shot the very day of his arrival.

"*June* 10.—Hans was ordered yesterday to hunt in the

direction of the Esquimaux huts, in the hope of determining the position of the open water. He did not return last night; but Dr Hayes and Mr Ohlsen, who were sent after him this morning with the dog-sledge, found the hardy savage fast asleep not five miles from the brig. Alongside of him was a large usuk or bearded seal, shot, as usual, in the head. He had dragged it for seven hours over the ice-foot. The dogs having now recruited, he started light to join Morton at the glacier.

"*June* 16.—Two long-tailed ducks visited us, evidently seeking their breeding-grounds. They are beautiful birds, either at rest or on the wing. We now have the snow-birds, the snipe, the burgomaster-gull, and the long-tailed duck, enlivening our solitude; but the snow-birds are the only ones in numbers, crowding our rocky islands, and making our sunny night-time musical with home-remembered songs. Of each of the others we have but a solitary pair, who seem to have left their fellows for this far northern mating-ground in order to live unmolested. I long for specimens; but they shall not be fired at.

"*June* 18.—Mr Ohlsen and Dr Hayes are off on an overland tramp. I sent them to inspect the open water to the southward. The immovable state of the ice-foot gives me anxiety. Last year, a large bay above us was closed all summer; and the land-ice, as we find it here, is as perennial as the glacier.

"*June* 21.—A snow, moist and flaky, melting upon our decks, and cleaning up the dingy surface of the great ice-plain with a new garment. We are at the summer solstice, the day of greatest solar light! Would that the traditionally-verified but meteorologically-disproved equinoctial storm could break upon us, to destroy the tenacious floes!

"*June* 22.—The ice changes slowly, but the progress of

vegetation is excessively rapid. The growth on the rocky group near our brig is surprising.

"*June* 23.—The eiders have come back: a pair were seen in the morning, soon followed by four ducks and drakes. The poor things seemed to be seeking breeding-grounds, but the ice must have scared them. They were flying southward.

"*June* 25.—Walked on shore and watched the changes: andromeda in flower, poppy and ranunculus the same: saw two snipe and some tern.

"Mr Ohlsen returned from a walk with Mr Petersen. They saw reindeer, and brought back a noble specimen of the king duck. It was a solitary male, resplendent with the orange, black, and green of his head and neck.

"Stephenson is better; and I think that a marked improvement, although a slow one, shows itself in all of us."

CHAPTER X.

THE NORTH-EAST PARTY.

"*June* 27.—M'Gary and Bonsall are back with Hickey and Riley. They arrived last evening: all well, except that the snow has affected their eyesight badly, owing to the scorbutic condition of their systems. Mr M'Gary is entirely blind, and I fear will be found slow to cure. They have done admirably. They bring back a continued series of observations, perfectly well kept up, for the further authentication of our survey, and their results correspond entirely with those of Mr Sontag and myself. They are connected, too, with the station at Chimney Rock, Cape Thackeray, which we have established by theodolite. I may be satisfied now with our projection of the Greenland coast. The different localities to the south have been referred to the position of our winter harbour, and this has been definitely fixed by the labours of Mr Sontag, our astronomer. We have, therefore, not only a reliable base, but a set of primary triangulations, which, though limited, may support the minor field-work of our sextants.

"M'Gary and Bonsall left the brig on the 3d, and reached the Great Glacier on the 15th, after only twelve days of travel. They showed great judgment in passing the bays; and, although impeded by the heavy snows, would have been able to remain much longer in the field, but for the destruction of our provision-depôts by the bears.

"This is evidently the season when the bears are in most abundance. Their tracks were everywhere, both on shore and upon the floes. One of them had the audacity to attempt intruding itself upon the party during one of their halts upon the ice; and Bonsall tells a good story of the manner in which they received and returned his salutations. It was about half an hour after midnight, and they were all sleeping away a long day's fatigue, when M'Gary either heard or felt, he could hardly tell which, something that was scratching at the snow immediately by his head. It waked him just enough to allow him to recognise a huge animal actively engaged in reconnoitring the circuit of the tent. His startled outcry aroused his companion-inmates, but without in any degree disturbing the unwelcome visitor; specially unwelcome at that time and place, for all the guns had been left on the sledge, a little distance off, and there was not so much as a walking-pole inside. There was, of course, something of natural confusion in the little council of war. The first impulse was to make a rush for the arms; but this was soon decided to be very doubtfully practicable, if at all; for the bear, having satisfied himself with his observations of the exterior, now presented himself at the tent-opening. Sundry volleys of lucifer matches and some impromptu torches of newspaper were fired without alarming him, and, after a little while, he planted himself at the doorway and began making his supper upon the carcass of a seal which had been shot the day before.

"Tom Hickey was the first to bethink him of the military device of a sortie from the postern, and, cutting a hole with his knife, crawled out at the rear of the tent. Here he extricated a boat-hook, that formed one of the supporters of the ridge-pole, and made it the instrument of a right valorous attack. A blow well administered on the nose caused the animal to retreat for the moment a few paces beyond the sledge, and Tom, calculating his distance nicely, sprang forward, seized a rifle, and fell back in safety upon his comrades. In a few seconds more, Mr Bonsall had sent a ball through and through the body of his enemy. I was assured that after this adventure the party adhered to the custom I had enjoined, of keeping at all times a watch and fire-arms inside the camping-tent.

"The final *cache*, which I relied so much upon, was entirely destroyed. It had been built, with extreme care, of rocks which had been assembled by very heavy labour, and adjusted with much aid often from capstan-bars as levers. The entire construction was, so far as our means permitted, most effective and resisting. Yet these tigers of the ice seemed to have scarcely encountered an obstacle.

Not a morsel of pemmican remained except in the iron cases, which, being round with conical ends, defied both claw and teeth. They had rolled and pawed them in every direction, tossing them about like foot-balls, although over eighty pounds in weight. An alcohol-case, strongly iron-bound, was dashed into small fragments, and a tin can of liquor mashed and twisted almost into a ball. The claws of the beast had perforated the metal, and torn it up as with a cold chisel.

"They were too dainty for salt-meats: ground coffee they had an evident relish for: old canvas was a favourite for some reason or other; even our flag, which had been reared 'to take possession' of the waste, was gnawed down to the very staff. They had made a regular frolic of it; rolling our bread-barrels over the ice-foot and into the broken outside ice; and, unable to masticate our heavy India-rubber cloth, they had tied it up in unimaginable hard knots.

"M'Gary describes the whole area around the *cache* as marked by the well-worn paths of these animals; and an adjacent slope of ice-covered rock, with an angle of 45°, was so worn and covered with their hair, as to suggest the idea that they had been amusing themselves by sliding down it on their haunches—a performance, by the way, in which I afterward caught them myself.

"*June* 28.—Hans came up with the party on the 17th. Morton and he are still out. They took a day's rest; and then, 'following the old tracks,' as M'Gary reports, 'till they were clear of the cracks near the islands, pushed northward at double-quick time. When last seen, they were both of them walking, for the snow was too soft and deep for them to ride with their heavy load.' Fine weather, but the ice yields reluctantly."

While thus watching the indications of advancing summer, my mind turned anxiously to the continued absence of Morton and Hans. We were already beyond the season when travel upon the ice was considered practicable by our English predecessors in Wellington Channel, and, in spite of the continued solidity around us, it was unsafe to presume too much upon our high northern position.

It was, therefore, with no slight joy that on the evening of the 10th, while walking with Mr Bonsall, a distant sound of dogs caught my ear. These faithful servants generally bayed their full-mouthed welcome from afar off, but they always dashed in with a wild speed which made their outcry a direct precursor of their arrival. Not so these well-worn travellers. Hans and Morton staggered beside the limping dogs, and poor Jenny was riding as a passenger upon the sledge. It was many hours before they shared the rest and comfort of our ship.

Mr Morton left the brig with the relief party of M'Gary on the 4th of June. He took his place at the track-lines like the others; but he was ordered to avoid all extra labour, so as to husband his strength for the final passage of the ice.

On the 15th he reached the base of the Great Glacier, and on the 16th was joined by Hans with the dogs. A single day was given to feed and refresh the animals, and on the 18th the two companies parted. Morton's account I give as nearly as possible in his own words, without affecting any modification of his style.

The party left Cache Island at 12.35 A.M., crossing the land-ices by portage, and going south for about a mile to avoid a couple of bad seams caused by the breakage of the glacier. Here Morton and Hans separated from the land-party, and went northward, keeping parallel with the glacier, and from five to seven miles distant. The ice was free from hummocks, but heavily covered with snow, through which they walked knee deep. They camped about eight miles from the glacier.

They started again at half-past nine. The ice at first was very heavy, and they were frequently over their knees in the dry snow; but, after crossing certain drifts, it became hard enough to bear the sledge, and the dogs made four miles an hour until twenty minutes past four, when they reached the middle of Peabody Bay. They then found themselves among the bergs which on former occasions had prevented other parties from getting through. These were generally very high, evidently newly separated from the glacier.

It took them a long while to get through into smoother ice. A tolerably wide passage would appear between two bergs, which they would gladly follow; then a narrower one; then no opening in front, but one to the side. Following that a little distance, a blank ice-cliff would close the way altogether, and they were forced to retrace their steps and begin again. Constantly baffled, but, like true fellows, determined to "go ahead," they at last found a lane some six miles to the west, which led upon their right course. But they were from eight o'clock at night till two or three the next morning, puzzling their way out of the maze, like a blind man in the streets of a strange city.

June 19.—At 8.45 A.M. they encamped. Again starting, they went on for ten miles, but were then arrested by wide seams in the ice, bergs, and much broken ice; so they turned about, and reached their last camp by twelve, midnight. They then went westward, and, after several trials, made a way, the dogs running well. It took them but two hours to reach the better ice, for the bergs were in a narrow belt.

They were now nearly abreast of the termination of the Great Glacier. It was mixed with earth and rocks. The snow sloped from the land to the ice, and the two seemed to be mingled together for eight or ten miles to the north, when the land became solid, and the glacier was lost. The height of this land seemed about 400 feet, and the glacier lower.

June 21.—They stood to the north at 11.30 P.M., and made for what Morton thought a cape, seeing a vacancy between it and the West Land. The ice was good, even, and free from bergs, only two or three being in sight. The atmosphere became thick and misty, and the west shore, which they saw faintly on Tuesday, was not visible. They could only see the cape for which they steered. The cold was sensibly felt, a very cutting wind blowing north-east by north. They reached the opening seen to the westward of the cape by Thursday, 7 A.M. It proved to be a channel; for, as they moved on in the misty weather, a sudden lifting of the fog showed them the cape and the western shore.

The ice was weak and rotten, and the dogs began to tremble. Proceeding at a brisk rate, they had got upon unsafe ice before they were aware of it. Their course was at the time nearly up the middle of the channel; but, as soon as possible, they turned, and, by a backward circuit, reached the shore. The dogs, as their fashion is, at first lay down and refused to proceed, trembling violently. The only way to induce the terrified, obstinate brutes to get on was for Hans to go to a white-looking spot where the ice was thicker, the soft stuff looking dark; then, calling the dogs coaxingly by name, they would crawl to him on their bellies. So they retreated from place to place, until they reached the firm ice they had quitted. A half-mile brought them to comparatively safe ice, a mile more to good ice again.

In the midst of this danger they had during the liftings of the fog sighted open water, and they now saw it plainly. There was no wind stirring, and its face was perfectly smooth. It was two miles further up the channel than the firm ice to which they had retreated. Hans could hardly believe it. But for the birds that were seen in great numbers, Morton says he would not have believed it himself.

The ice covered the mouth of the channel like a horse-shoe. One end lapped into the west side a considerable distance up the channel, the other covered the cape for about a mile and a half, so that they could not land opposite their camp, which was about a mile and a half from the cape.

That night they succeeded in climbing on to the level by the floe-pieces, and walked around the turn of the cape for some distance, leaving their dogs behind. They found a good ice-foot, very wide, which extended as far as the cape.

They started again at 11.30 A.M. of the 21st. On reaching the land-ice, they unloaded, and threw each package of provision from the floe up to the ice-foot, which was eight or nine feet above them. Morton then climbed up with the aid of the sledge, which they converted into a ladder for the occasion. He then pulled the dogs up by the lines fastened round their bodies, Hans lending a helping hand and then climbing up himself. They then drew up the sledge. The water was very deep,—a stone the size of Morton's head taking twenty-eight seconds to reach the bottom, which was seen very clearly.

As they had noticed the night before, the ice-foot lost

its good character on reaching the cape, becoming a mere narrow ledge hugging the cliffs, and looking as if it might crumble off altogether into the water at any moment. Morton was greatly afraid there would be no land-ice there at all when they came back. Hans and he thought they might pass on by climbing along the face of the crag; in fact they tried a path about fifty feet high, but it grew so narrow that they saw they could not get the dogs past with their sledge-load of provisions. He therefore thought it safest to leave some food, that they might not starve on the return in case the ice-foot should disappear. He accordingly *cached* enough provision to last them back, with four days' dog-meat.

At the pitch of the cape the ice-ledge was hardly three feet wide; and they were obliged to unloose the dogs and drive them forward alone. Hans and he then tilted the sledge up, and succeeded in carrying it past the narrowest place. The ice-foot was firm under their tread, though it crumbled on the verge.

They now yoked in the dogs, and set forward over the worst sort of mashed ice for three-quarters of a mile. After passing the cape, they looked ahead, and saw nothing but open water. After turning the cape, they found a good smooth ice-foot in the entering curve of a bay. They came upon glassy ice, and the dogs ran on it full speed. Here the sledge made at least six miles an hour. It was the best day's travel they made on the journey.

The part of the channel they were now coasting was narrower, but as they proceeded it seemed to widen again.

To the left of this, toward the West Land, the great channel of open water continued. There was broken ice floating in it, but with passages fifteen miles in width and perfectly clear. The end of the point—"Gravel Point," as Morton called it—was covered with hummocks and broken ice for about two miles from the water. This ice was worn and full of gravel. Six miles inland the point was flanked by mountains.

The wind blew strong from the north, and continued to do so for three days, sometimes blowing a gale, and very damp, the tops of the hills becoming fixed with dark foggy clouds. The damp falling mist prevented their seeing any distance. Yet they saw no ice borne down from the northward during all this time; and, what was more curious, they found, on their return south, that no ice had been sent down during the gale. On the contrary, they then found the channel perfectly clear from shore to shore.

June 22.—They camped at 8.30 A.M. on a ledge of low rock, having made in the day's journey forty-eight miles in a straight line.

June 23.—In consequence of the gale of wind they did not start till 12.30 midnight. They made about eight miles, and were arrested by the broken ice of the shore. Their utmost efforts could not pass the sledge over this; so they tied the dogs to it, and went ahead to see how things looked. They found the land-ice growing worse and worse, until at last it ceased, and the water broke directly against the steep cliffs.

June 23.—At 3 A.M. they started again, carrying eight pounds of pemmican and two of bread, besides the artificial horizon, sextant, and compass, a rifle, and the boat-hook. After two hours' walking the travel improved, and, on nearing a plain about nine miles from where they had left the sledge, they were rejoiced to see a she-bear and her cub. They had tied the dogs securely, as they thought; but Toodla and four others had broken loose and followed them, making their appearance within an hour. They were thus able to attack the bear at once.

Hans, who to the simplicity of an Esquimaux united the shrewd observation of a hunter, describes the contest which followed so graphically, that I try to engraft some of the quaintness of his description upon Mr Morton's report. The bear fled; but the little one being unable either to keep ahead of the dogs or to keep pace with her, she turned back, and putting her head under its haunches, threw it some distance ahead. The cub safe for the moment, she would wheel round and face the dogs, so as to give it a chance to run away; but it always stopped just as it alighted, till she came up and threw it ahead again: it seemed to expect her aid, and would not go on without it. Sometimes the mother would run a few yards ahead, as if to coax the young one up to her, and when the dogs came up she would turn on them and drive them back; then, as they dodged her blows, she would rejoin the cub and push it on, sometimes putting her head under it, sometimes catching it in her mouth by the nape of the neck.

For a time she managed her retreat with great celerity, leaving the two men far in the rear. They had engaged her on the land-ice; but she led the dogs in-shore, up a small stony valley which opened into the interior. But, after she had gone a mile and a half, her pace slackened, and, the little one being jaded, she soon came to a halt.

The men were then only half a mile behind; and, running at full speed, they soon came up to where the dogs were holding her at bay. The fight was now a desperate one. The mother never went more than two yards ahead, constantly looking at the cub. When the dogs came near her, she would sit upon her haunches and take the little one between her hind legs, fighting the dogs with her

Far North—*Page* 111.

paws, and roaring so that she could have been heard a mile off. "Never," said Morton, "was an animal more distressed." She would stretch her neck and snap at the nearest dog with her shining teeth, whirling her paws like the arms of a windmill. If she missed her aim, not daring to pursue one dog lest the others should harm the cub, she would give a great roar of baffled rage, and go on pawing, and snapping, and facing the ring, grinning at them with her mouth stretched wide.

When the men came up, the little one was perhaps rested, for it was able to turn round with her dam, no matter how quick she moved, so as to keep always in front of her belly. The five dogs were all the time frisking about her actively, tormenting her like so many gad-flies; indeed, they made it difficult to lodge a bullet in her without killing them. But Hans, lying on his elbow, took a quiet aim and shot her through the head. She dropped and rolled over dead without moving a muscle.

The dogs sprang toward her at once; but the cub jumped upon her body and reared up, for the first time growling hoarsely. They seemed quite afraid of the little creature, she fought so actively and made so much noise; and, while tearing mouthfuls of hair from the dead mother, they would spring aside the minute the cub turned toward them. The men drove the dogs off for a time, but were obliged to shoot the cub at last, as she would not quit the body.

Hans fired into her head. It did not reach the brain, though it knocked her down; but she was still able to climb on her mother's body and try to defend it still, "her mouth bleeding like a gutter-spout." They were obliged to despatch her with stones.

After skinning the old one they gashed its body, and the

dogs fed upon it ravenously. The little one they *cached* for themselves on the return; and, with difficulty taking the dogs off, pushed on, crossing a small bay which extended from the level ground and had still some broken ice upon it. Hans was tired out, and was sent on shore to follow the curve of the bay, where the road was easier.

Morton tried to pass round the cape. It was in vain: there was no ice-foot; and, trying his best to ascend the cliffs, he could get up but a few hundred feet. Here he fastened to his walking-pole the Grinnell flag of the *Antarctic*—a well-cherished little relic, which had now followed me on two Polar voyages. This flag had been saved from the wreck of the United States sloop-of-war *Peacock*, when she stranded off the Columbia River; it had accompanied Commodore Wilkes in his far southern discovery of an Antarctic continent. It was now its strange destiny to float over the highest northern land, not only of America, but of our globe. Side by side with this were our masonic emblems of the compass and the square. He let them fly for an hour and a half from the black cliff over the dark rock-shadowed waters, which rolled up and broke in white caps at its base.

Beyond this cape all is surmise. The high ridges to the north-west dwindled off into low blue knobs, which blended finally with the air. Morton called the cape, which baffled his labours, after his commander; but I have given it the more enduring name of Cape Constitution.

He was bitterly disappointed that he could not get round the cape, to see whether there was any land beyond; but it was impossible. Rejoining Hans, they supped off their bread and pemmican, and, after a good nap, started on their return on the 25th, at 1.30 P.M.

CHAPTER XI.

ATTEMPT TO REACH BEECHY ISLAND.

ALL the sledge-parties were now once more aboard ship, and the season of Arctic travel had ended. For more than two months we had been imprisoned in ice, and throughout all that period, except during the enforced holiday of the midwinter darkness, or while repairing from actual disaster, had been constantly in the field. The summer was wearing on, but still the ice did not break up as it should. As far as we could see, it remained inflexibly solid between us and the North Water of Baffin's Bay. The questions and speculations of those around me began to show that they too had anxious thoughts for the coming year. There was reason for all our apprehensions, as some of my notes may show.

"*July* 8.—Penny saw water to the southward in Barrow's Straits as early as June; and by the first of July the leads were within a mile of his harbour in Wellington Channel. Dr Sutherland says he could have cut his way out by the 15th. Austin was not liberated till the 10th of August; but the water had worked up to within three miles and a half of him as early as the 1st, having advanced twenty miles in the preceding month. If, now, we might assume that the ice between us and the nearest water would give way as rapidly as it did in these two cases,— an assumption, by the way, which the difference of the localities is all against, the mouth of our harbour should be reached in fifty days, or by the last day of August; and after that, several days, or perhaps weeks, must go by before the inside ice yields around our brig.

"I know by experience how soon the ice breaks up after it once begins to go, and I hardly think that it can continue advancing so slowly much longer. Indeed, I look for it to open, if it opens at all, about the beginning of September at furthest, somewhere near the date of Sir James Ross's liberation at Leopold. But then I have to remember that I am much further to the north than my predecessors, and that by the 28th of last August I had already, after twenty days of unremitting labour, forced the brig nearly forty miles through the pack, and that the pack began to close on us only six days later, and that on the 7th of September we were fairly frozen in. Yet last summer was a most favourable one for ice-melting. Putting all this together, it looks as if the winter must catch us before we can get half-way through the pack, even though we should begin warping to the south at the earliest moment that we can hope for water.

"It is not a pleasant conclusion of the argument; for there never was, and I trust never will be, a party worse armed for the encounter of a second Arctic winter. We have neither health, fuel, nor provisions. Dr Hayes, and indeed all I have consulted about it indirectly, despond at the thought; and when I look round upon our diseased and disabled men, and think of the fearful work of the last long night, I am tempted to feel as they do.

"The alternative of abandoning the vessel at this early stage of our absence, even were it possible, would, I feel, be dishonouring; but, revolving the question as one of practicability alone, I would not undertake it. In the first place, how are we to get along with our sick and newly-amputated men? It is a dreary distance at the best to Upernavik or Beechy Island, our only seats of refuge, and a precarious traverse if we were all of us fit for moving, but we are hardly one-half in efficiency of what we count in number. Besides, how can I desert the brig while there is still a chance of saving her? There is no use of noting *pros* and *cons:* my mind is made up; I will not do it.

"But I must examine this ice-field for myself. I have been maturing through the last fortnight a scheme of relief, based upon a communication with the English squadron to the south, and to-morrow I set out to reconnoitre. Hans will go with me. We will fit out our poor travel-worn dogs with canvas shoes, and cross the floes to the true water edge, or at least be satisfied that it is impossible. 'He sees best who uses his own eyes.'

"*July* 11.—We got back last night: a sixty miles' journey,—comfortless enough, with only three hours' sleep on the ice. For thirty-five miles south, the straits are absolutely tight. Off Refuge Inlet and Esquimaux Point we found driving leads; but between these points and the brig not a crack. I pushed the dogs over the drift-ice, and, after a fair number of mischances, found the North Water. It was flowing and free; but since M'Gary saw it last May it has not advanced more than four miles. It would be absurd at this season of the year to attempt escaping in open boats with this ice between us and water. All that can be done is to reinforce our energies as we may, and look the worst in the face.

"In view of these contingencies, I have determined to attempt in person to communicate with Beechy Island, or at least make the effort. If I can reach Sir Edward Belcher's squadron, I am sure of all I want. I will take a light whale-boat, and pick my companions for a journey to the south and west. I may find perhaps the stores of the *North Star* at the Wostenholm Islands, or by great good luck come across some passing vessel of the squadron, and make known our whereabouts and wants; or, failing these, we will try and coast it along to Wellington Channel.

"A depôt of provisions, and a seaworthy craft large enough to carry us—if I had these, everything would be right. Even Sir John Ross's launch, the *Little Mary*, that he left at Union Bay, would serve our purpose. If I had her I could make a southern passage after the fall-tides. The great enemy of that season is the young shore-ice, that would cut through our frail boats like a saw. Or, if we can only renew our stock of provisions for the winter, we may await the chances of next year.

"As a prelude to this solemn undertaking, I met my officers in the evening, and showed them my ice-charts; explaining, what I found needed little explanation, the prospect immediately before us. I then discussed the probable changes, and, giving them my personal opinion that the brig might after all be liberated at a later date, I announced my project. I will not say how gratified I was with the manner in which they received it. It struck me that there was a sense of personal relief experienced everywhere. I told them that I did not choose to call a council or connect any of them with the responsibilities of the measure, for it involved only the personal safety of those who chose to share the risk. Full instructions were then left for their guidance during my absence.

"It was the pleasantest interview I ever had with my associates. I believe every man on board would have volunteered, but I confined myself to five active men: James M'Gary, William Morton, George Riley, Hans Christian, and Thomas Hickey, made up my party."

Our equipment had been getting ready for some time, though without its object being understood or announced.

The boat was our old *Forlorn Hope*, mended up and revised for her new destinies.

Morton, who was in my confidence from the first, had all our stores ready. We had no game, and no meat but pork, of which we took some hundred and fifty pounds. I wanted pemmican, and sent the men out in search of the cases which were left on the floe by the frozen depôt-party during the rescue of last March; but they could not find a trace of them, or indeed of anything else we abandoned at that time—a proof, if we wanted one, how blurred all our faculties must have been by suffering, for we marked them, as we thought, with marvellous care.

We lifted our boat over the side in the afternoon, and floated her to the crack at the Observatory Island; mounted her there on our large sledge *The Faith*, by an arrangement of cradles of Mr Ohlsen's devising; stowed in everything but the provisions, and carried her on to the bluff of Sylvia Headland; and the next morning a party, consisting of all but the sick, was detailed to transport her to open water; while M'Gary, Hans, and myself, followed with our *St John's* sledge, carrying our stores.

In four days more we had carried the boat across twenty miles of heavy ice-floe, and launched her in open water.

The straits were much clogged with drift, but I followed the coast southward without difficulty. We travelled at night, resting when the sun was hottest. I had every reason to be pleased with the performance of the whale-boat, and the men kept up their spirits well. We landed at the point where we left our life-boat a year ago, and to our great joy found it untouched: the cove and inlet were still fast in ice.

We now neared Littleton Island, where a piece of good fortune awaited us. We saw a number of ducks, both eiders and heraldas; and it occurred to me that by tracking their flight we should reach their breeding-grounds. There was no trouble in doing so, for they flew in a straight line to a group of rocky islets, above which the whole horizon was studded with birds. A rugged little ledge, which I named Eider Island, was so thickly colonised that we could hardly walk without treading on a nest. We killed with guns and stones over two hundred birds in a few hours.

We camped at this nursery of wild fowl, and laid in four large India-rubber bags full, cleaned and rudely boned. Our boat was hauled up and refitted; and, the trial having shown us that she was too heavily laden for safety, I made a general reduction of our stores, and *cached* the surplus under the rocks.

On the 19th we left Flagstaff Point, where we fixed our beacon last year; and stood west 10° south under full canvas. My aim was to take the channel obliquely at Littleton Island; and, making the drift-ice or the land to the south-west in the neighbourhood of Cape Combermere, push on for Kent Island and leave a cairn there.

Toward night the wind freshened from the northward, and we passed beyond the protection of the straits into the open sea-way. My journal gives no picture of the life we now entered on. The oldest sailor who treads the deck of his ship with the familiar confidence of a man at home, has a distrust of open-boat navigation which a landsman hardly shares. The feeling grew upon us as we lost the land. M'Gary was an old Behring's Straits whaler, and there is no better boatman in the world than he; but I know that he shared my doubts, as the boat buried herself again and again in the trough of a short chopping sea, which it taxed all his dexterity in steering to meet.

Baffin passed around this gulf in 1616 with two small vessels; but they were giants beside ours. I thought of them as we crossed his track steering for Cape Combermere, then about sixty miles distant, with every prospect of a heavy gale.

We were in the centre of this large area of open water when the gale broke upon us from the north. We were near foundering. Our false bow of India-rubber cloth was beaten in, and our frail weather-boarding soon followed it. With the utmost exertion we could hardly keep our boat from broaching to: a broken oar or an accidental twitch would have been fatal to us at any time. But M'Gary handled that whaler's marvel, the long steering-oar, with admirable skill. None of us could pretend to take his place. For twenty-two unbroken hours he stuck to his post without relaxing his attention or his efforts.

I was not prepared for such a storm. I do not think I have seen a worse sea raised by the northern wind of the Gulf of Mexico. At last the wind hauled to the eastward, and we were glad to drive before it for the in-shore floes. We had passed several bergs; but the sea dashed against their sides so furiously as to negative all hope of protection at their base; the pack or floe, so much feared before, was now looked to for a refuge.

I remember well our anxiety as we entered the loose streams of drift after four hours' scudding, and our relief when we felt their influence upon the sea. We fastened to an old floe, not fifty yards in diameter, and, with the weather-surf breaking over our heads, rode out the storm under a warp and grapnel.

The obstacle we had now to encounter was the pack that stretched between us and the south.

When the storm abated we commenced boring into it,

—slow work at the best of times; but my companions encountered it with a persevering activity quite as admirable as their fortitude in danger. It had its own hazards too; and more than once it looked as if we were permanently beset. I myself knew that we might rely on the southerly wind to liberate us from such an imprisonment; but I saw that the men thought otherwise, as the ice-fields closed around us and the horizon showed an unchanging circle of ice.

A slackening of the ice to the east enabled us after a while to lay our course for Hakluyt Island. We spread our canvas again, and reached the in-shore fields by one in the afternoon. We made our camp, dried our buffalo-skins, and sunned and slept away our fatigue.

We renewed our labours in the morning. Keeping inside the pack, we coasted along for the Cary Islands, encountering now and then a projecting floe, and either boring or passing around it, but making a satisfactory progress on the whole toward Lancaster Sound.

For the next three days we worked painfully through the half-open leads, making in all some fifteen miles to the south. We had very seldom room enough to row; but, as we tracked along, it was not difficult to escape nippings, by hauling up the boat on the ice. Still she received some hard knocks, and a twist or two that did not help her sea-worthiness, for she began to leak; and this, with the rain which fell heavily, forced us to bale her out every other hour. Of course we could not sleep, and one of our little party fell sick with the unmitigated fatigue.

On the 29th it came on to blow, the wind still keeping from the south-west, but cold and almost rising to a gale. We had had another wet and sleepless night, for the floes still baffled us by their capricious movements. But at three in the afternoon we had the sun again, and the ice opened just enough to tempt us. It was uncomfortable toil. We pushed forward our little weather-worn craft, her gunwales touching on both sides, till the toppling ice began to break down on us, and sometimes, critically suspended, met above our heads.

One of these passages I am sure we all of us remember. We were in an alley of pounded ice-masses, such as the receding floes leave when they have crushed the tables that were between them, and had pushed our way far enough to make retreat impossible, when the fields began to close in. There was no escaping a nip, for everything was loose and rolling around us, and the floes broke into hummock-ridges as they came together. They met just ahead of us, and gradually swayed in toward our boat. The fragments were already splitting off and spinning over us, when we found ourselves borne up by the accumulating rubbish, like the *Advance* in her winter drift; and, after resting for twenty minutes high out of water, quietly lowered again as the fields relaxed their pressure.

Generally, however, the ice-fields came together directly, and so gradually as to enable us to anticipate their contact. In such cases, as we were short-handed and our boat heavily laden, we were glad to avail ourselves of the motion of the floes to assist in lifting her upon them. We threw her across the lead by a small pull of the steering-oar, and let her meet the approaching ice upon her bow. The effect, as we found in every instance, was to press her down forward as the floe advanced against her, and to raise her stern above the level of the other field. We held ourselves ready for the spring as she began to rise.

It was a time of almost unbroken excitement; yet I am not surprised, as I turn over the notes of my meagre diary, to find how little of stirring incident it records. The story of one day's strife with the ice-floes might also serve for those which followed it. I remember that we were four times nipped before we succeeded in releasing ourselves, and that we were glad to haul upon the floes as often as a dozen times a day. We attempted to drag forward on the occasional fields; but we had to give it up, for it strained the boat so much that she was barely sea-worthy; it kept one man busy the last six days bailing her out.

On the 31st, at the distance of ten miles from Cape Parry, we came to a dead halt. A solid mass lay directly across our path, extending onward to our furthest horizon. There were bergs in sight to the westward, and by walking for some four miles over the moving floe in that direction, M'Gary and myself succeeded in reaching one. We climbed it to the height of a hundred and twenty feet, and, looking out from it with my excellent spy-glass to the south and west, we saw that all within a radius of thirty miles was a motionless, unbroken, and impenetrable sea.

I had not counted on this. I had met no ice here only seven days later in 1853. Yet it was plain, that from Cape Combermere on the west side, and an unnamed bay immediately to the north of it, across to Hakluyt Island, there extended a continuous barrier of ice. We had scarcely penetrated beyond its margin.

We had, in fact, reached the dividing pack of the two great open waters of Baffin's Bay. The experience of the whalers and of the expedition-ships that have traversed this region have made all of us familiar with that great expanse of open sea, to the north of Cape Dudley Diggs, which has received the name of the North Water. Combining the observations of Baffin, Ross, and Inglefield, we know that this sometimes extends as far north as Littleton Island, embracing an area of 90,000 square miles. The voyagers I have named could not, of course, be aware of the interesting fact that this water is divided, at least occasionally, into two distinct bodies; the one comprehended between Lancaster and Jones's Sounds, the other extending from the point we had now reached to the upper pack of Smith's Straits. But it was evident to all of our party that the barrier which now arrested us was made up of the ices which Jones's Sound on the west and Murchison's on the east had discharged and driven together.

It was obvious that a further attempt to penetrate to the south must be hopeless till the ice-barrier before us should undergo a change. I had observed, when passing Northumberland Island, that some of its glacier-slopes were margined with verdure, an almost unfailing indication of animal life; and, as my men were much wasted with diarrhœa, and our supplies of food had become scanty, I resolved to work my way to the island, and recruit there for another effort.

Tracking and sometimes rowing through a heavy rain, we traversed the leads for two days, working eastward; and on the morning of the third gained the open water near the shore. Here a breeze came to our aid, and in a couple of hours more we passed with now unwonted facility to the southern face of the island. We met several flocks of little auks as we approached it, and found on landing that it was one enormous homestead of the auks, dovekies, and gulls.

We encamped on the 31st, on a low beach at the foot of a moraine that came down between precipitous cliffs of surpassing wildness. It had evidently been selected by the Esquimaux for a winter settlement: five well-built huts of stone attested this. Three of them were still tolerably perfect, and bore marks of recent habitation. The droppings of the birds had fertilised the soil, and it abounded in grasses and sorrel to the water's edge. The foxes were about in great numbers, attracted, of course, by the abundance of birds. They were all of them of the lead-coloured variety, without a white one among them. The young ones, as yet lean and seemingly unskilled in hospitable courtesies, barked at us as we walked about.

CHAPTER XII.

THE SECOND WINTER—DEPARTURE OF HALF OF THE CREW.

It was with mingled feelings that we neared the brig Our little party had grown fat and strong upon the auks and eiders and scurvy-grass; and surmises were rife among us as to the condition of our comrades and the prospects of our ice-bound ship.

The tide-leads, which one year ago had afforded a precarious passage to the vessel, now barely admitted our whale-boat; and, as we forced her through the broken ice, she showed such signs of hard usage, that I had her hauled up upon the land-belt and housed under the cliffs at Six-mile Ravine. We crossed the rocks on foot, aided by our jumping-poles, and startled our shipmates by our sudden appearance.

In the midst of the greeting which always met our

returning parties, and which gave to our little vessel the endearing associations of a homestead, our thoughts reverted to the feeble chances of our liberation, and the failure of our recent effort to secure the means of a retreat.

The brig had been imprisoned by closely-cementing ice for eleven months, during which period she had not budged an inch from her icy cradle.

"*August* 8.—This morning two saw-lines were passed from the open-water pools at the sides of our stern-post, and the ice was bored for blasting. In the course of our operations the brig surged and righted, rising two and a half feet. We are now trying to warp her a few yards toward Butler Island, where we again go to work with our powder-canisters. The blasting succeeded; one canister cracked and uplifted 200 square yards of ice with but five pounds of powder. A prospect showed itself of getting inside the island at high water; and I determined to attempt it at the highest spring-tide, which takes place on the 12th.

"*August* 12.—The brig bore the strain of her new position very well. The tide fell fifteen feet, leaving her high and dry; but, as the water rose, everything was replaced, and the deck put in order for warping again. Every one in the little vessel turned to; and after much excitement, at the very top of the tide, she passed 'by the skin of her teeth.' She was then warped in a bight of the floe, near Fox-Trap Point, and there she now lies.

" We congratulated ourselves upon effecting this crossing. Had we failed, we should have had to remain fast probably for the high tides a fortnight hence. The young ice is already forming, and our hopes rest mainly upon the late gales of August and September.

"*August* 15.—To-day I made another ice-inspection to

the north-east. The floe on which I have trudged so often, the big bay-floe of our former mooring, is nearly the same as when we left it. I recognised the holes and cracks, through the fog, by a sort of instinct. M'Gary and myself had little difficulty in reaching the Fiord Water by our jumping-poles.

"I have my eye on this water, for it may connect with the north-east headland, and hereafter give us a passage.

"The season travels on: the young ice grows thicker, and my messmates' faces grow longer every day. I have again to play buffoon to keep up the spirits of the party.

"A raven! The snow-birds begin to fly to the south in groups, coming at night to our brig to hover on the rigging. Winter is hurrying upon us. The poppies are quite wilted.

"Examined ice with Mr Bonsall, and determined to enter the broken land-ices by warping; not that there is the slightest probability of getting through, but it affords moral aid and comfort to the men and officers: it looks as if we were doing something.

"*August* 17.—Warped about 100 yards into the trash, and, after a long day of labour, have turned in, hoping to recommence at 5 A.M. to-morrow.

"In five days the spring-tides come back; should we fail in passing with them, I think our fortunes are fixed. The young ice bore a man this morning: it had a bad look, this man-supporting August ice! The temperature never falls below 28°; but it is cold o' nights with no fire.

"*August* 18.—Reduced our allowance of wood to six pounds a meal. This, among eighteen mouths, is one-third of a pound of fuel for each. It allows us coffee twice a day, and soup once. Our fare besides this is cold pork

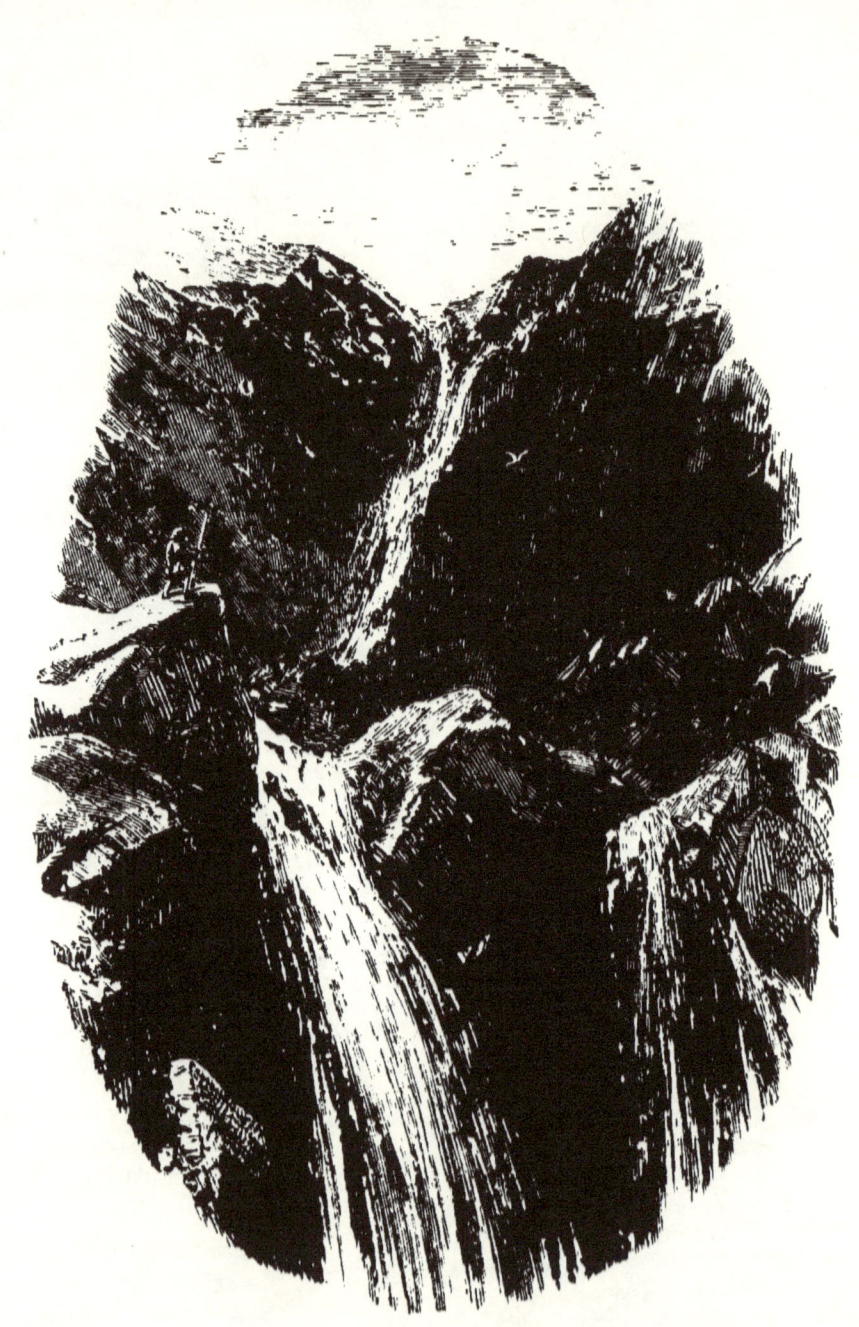

Far North. *Page 147.*

boiled in quantity and eaten as required. This sort of thing works badly; but I must save coal for other emergencies. I see 'darkness ahead.'

"I inspected the ice again to-day. Bad! bad!—I must look another winter in the face. I do not shrink from the thought; but, while we have a chance ahead, it is my first duty to have all things in readiness to meet it. It is *horrible*—yes, that is the word!—to look forward to another year of disease and darkness, to be met without fresh food and without fuel. I should meet it with a more tempered sadness if I had no comrades to think for and protect.

"*August* 20.—Rest for all hands. The daily prayer is no longer, 'Lord, accept our gratitude, and bless our undertaking,' but, 'Lord, accept our gratitude, and restore us to our homes.' The ice shows no change: after a boat and foot journey around the entire south-eastern curve of the bay, no signs!"

My attempt to reach Beechy Island had disclosed, as I thought it would, the impossibility of reaching the settlements of Greenland.

Everything before us was now involved in gloomy doubt. Hopeful as I had been, it was impossible not to feel that we were near the climax of the expedition.

I determined to place upon Observatory Island a large signal-beacon or cairn, and to bury under it documents which, in case of disaster to our party, would convey to any who might seek us intelligence of our proceedings and our fate. The memory of the first winter-quarters of Sir John Franklin, and the painful feelings with which, while standing by the graves of his dead, I had five years before sought for written signs pointing to the fate of the living, made me careful to avoid a similar neglect.

A conspicuous spot was selected upon a cliff looking

out upon the icy desert, and on a broad face of rock the words—

ADVANCE,
A.D. 1853-54,

were painted in letters which could be read at a distance. A pyramid of heavy stones, perched above it, was marked with the Christian symbol of the cross. It was not without a holier sentiment than that of mere utility that I placed under this the coffins of our two poor comrades. It was our beacon, and their gravestone.

Near this a hole was worked into the rock, and a paper, enclosed in glass, sealed in with melted lead. It read as follows:—

"BRIG 'ADVANCE,' *August* 14, 1854.

"E. K. Kane, with his comrades, Henry Brooks, John Wall Wilson, James M'Gary, I. I. Hayes, Christian Ohlsen, Amos Bonsall, Henry Goodfellow, August Sontag, William Morton, J. Carl Petersen, George Stephenson, Jefferson Temple Baker, George Riley, Peter Schubert, George Whipple, John Blake, Thomas Hickey, William Godfrey, and Hans Christian, members of the Second Grinnell Expedition in search of Sir John Franklin and the missing crews of the *Erebus* and *Terror*, were forced into this harbour while endeavouring to bore the ice to the north and east.

"They were frozen in on the 8th of September 1853, and liberated ———

"During this period the labours of the expedition have delineated 960 miles of coast-line, without developing any traces of the missing ships or the slightest information bearing upon their fate. The amount of travel to effect this exploration exceeded 2000 miles, all of which was upon foot or by the aid of dogs.

"Greenland has been traced to its northern face, whence it is connected with the further north of the opposite coast by a great glacier. This coast has been charted as high as lat. 82° 27'. Smith's Sound expands into a capacious bay: it has been surveyed throughout its entire extent. From its northern and eastern corner, in lat. 80° 10', long. 66°, a channel has been discovered and followed until further progress was checked by water free from ice. This channel trended nearly due north, and expanded into an apparently open sea, which abounded with birds and bears and marine life.

"The death of the dogs during the winter threw the travel essential to the above discoveries upon the personal efforts of the officers and men. The summer finds them much broken in health and strength.

"Jefferson Temple Baker and Peter Schubert died from injuries received from cold while in manly performance of their duty. Their remains are deposited under a cairn at the north point of Observatory Island.

"The site of the observatory is 76 English feet from the northernmost salient point of this island, in a direction south 14° east. Its position is in lat. 78° 37' 10", long. 70° 40'. The mean tidal level is 20 feet below the highest point upon this island. Both of these sites are further designated by copper bolts, sealed with melted lead into holes upon the rocks.

"On the 12th of August 1854, the brig warped from her position, and, after passing inside the group of islands, fastened to the outer floe about a mile to the north-west, where she is now awaiting further changes in the ice.

    (Signed) "E. K. KANE,
        "Commanding Expedition.

"Fox Trap Point, *August* 14, 1854."

The following note was added some hours later:—

"The young ice having formed between the brig and this island, and prospects of a gale showing themselves, the date of departure is left unfilled. If possible, a second visit will be made to insert our dates, our final escape being still dependent upon the course of the season.
"E. K. KANE."

And now came the question of the second winter—how to look our enemy in the face, and how to meet him. Anything was better than inaction; and, in spite of the uncertainty which yet attended our plans, a host of expedients were to be resorted to, and much Robinson Crusoe labour ahead. Moss was to be gathered for eking out our winter fuel, and willow-stems, and stonecrops, and sorrel, as antiscorbutics, collected and buried in the snow. But while all these were in progress came other and graver questions.

Some of my party had entertained the idea than an escape to the south was still practicable; and this opinion was supported by Mr Petersen, our Danish interpreter, who had accompanied the Searching Expedition of Captain Penny, and had a matured experience in the changes of Arctic ice. They even thought that the safety of all would be promoted by a withdrawal from the brig.

"*August* 21.—The question of detaching a party was in my mind some time ago; but the more I thought it over, the more I was convinced that it would be neither right in itself nor practically safe. For myself personally, it is a simple duty of honour to remain by the brig: I could not think of leaving her till I had proved the effect of the later tides; and after that, as I have known all along, it would be too late. Come what may, I share her fortunes.

"But it is a different question with my associates. I cannot expect them to adopt my impulses; and I am by no means sure that I ought to hold them bound by my conclusions. Have I the *moral right?* for, as to nautical rules, they do not fit the circumstances; among the whalers, when a ship is hopelessly beset, the master's authority gives way, and the crew take counsel for themselves whether to go or stay by her. My party is subordinate and well-disposed; but if the restlessness of suffering makes some of them anxious to brave the chances, they may certainly plead that a second winter in the ice was no part of the cruise they bargained for.

"But what presses on me is of another character. I cannot disguise it from myself that we are wretchedly prepared for another winter on board. We are a set of scurvy-riddled, broken-down men; our provisions are sorely reduced in quantity, and are altogether unsuited to our condition. My only hope of maintaining or restoring such a degree of health among us as is indispensable to our escape in the spring has been and must be in a wholesome, elastic tone of feeling among the men: a reluctant, brooding. disheartened spirit would sweep our decks like a pestilence. I fear the bane of depressing example.

"I know all this as a medical man and an officer; and I feel that we might be wearing away the hearts and energies, if not the lives of all, by forcing those who were reluctant to remain. With half a dozen confiding, resolute men, I have no fears of ultimate safety.

"I will make a thorough inspection of the ice to-morrow, and decide finally the prospects of our liberation.

"*August* 23.—The brig cannot escape. I got an eligible position with my sledge to review the floes, and returned this morning at two o'clock. There is no possibility of our release, unless by some extreme intervention of the coming tides. I doubt whether a boat could be forced as far as the Southern Water. When I think of the extraordinary way in which the ice was impacted last winter, how very little it has yielded through the summer, and how early another winter is making its onset upon us, I am very doubtful, indeed, whether our brig can get away at all. It would be inexpedient to attempt leaving her now in boats—the water-streams closing, the pack nearly fast again, and the young ice almost impenetrable.

"I shall call the officers and crew together, and make known to them very fully how things look, and what hazards must attend such an effort as has been proposed among them. They shall have my view unequivocally expressed. I will then give them twenty-four hours to deliberate; and at the end of that time all who determine to go shall say so in writing, with a full exposition of the circumstances of the case. They shall have the best outfit I can give, an abundant share of our remaining stores, and my good-bye blessing.

"*August* 24.—At noon to-day I had all hands called, and explained to them frankly the considerations which have determined me to remain where we are. I endeavoured to show them that an escape to open water could not succeed, and that the effort must be exceedingly hazardous: I alluded to our duties to the ship; in a word, I advised them strenuously to forego the project. I then told them that I should freely give my permission to such as were desirous of making the attempt, but that I should require them to place themselves under the command of officers selected by them before setting out, and to renounce in writing all claims upon myself and the rest who were resolved to stay by the vessel. Having done this, I directed the roll to be called, and each man to answer for himself."

In the result, eight out of the seventeen survivors of my party resolved to stand by the brig. It is just that I should record their names. They were Brooks, M'Gary, Wilson, Goodfellow, Morton, Ohlsen, Hickey, and Christian.

I divided to the others their portion of our resources justly and even liberally; and they left us on Monday, the 28th, with every appliance our narrow circumstances could furnish to speed and guard them. One of them, George Riley, returned a few days afterward; but weary months went by before we saw the rest again. They carried with them a written assurance of a brother's welcome should they be driven back; and this assurance was redeemed when hard trials had prepared them to share again our fortunes.

The party moved off with the elastic step of men confident in their purpose, and were out of sight in a few hours. As we lost them among the hummocks, the stern realities of our condition pressed themselves upon us anew. The reduced numbers of our party, the helplessness of many, the waning efficiency of all, the impending winter, with its cold dark night, our penury of resources, the dreary sense of increased isolation,—these made the staple of our thoughts. For a time Sir John Franklin and his party, our daily topic through so many months, gave place to the question of our own fortunes,—how we were to escape, how to live. The summer had gone, the harvest was ended, and—— We did not care to finish the sentence.

We were like men driven to the wall, quickened, not depressed. Our plans were formed at once: there is nothing like emergency to speed, if not to instruct, the energies.

It was my first definite resolve that, come what might, our organization and its routine of observances should be adhered to strictly. It is the experience of every man who has either combated difficulties himself, or attempted to guide others through them, that the controlling law shall be systematic action. Nothing depresses and demoralises so much as a surrender of the approved and habitual forms of life. I resolved that everything should go on as it had done. The arrangement of hours, the distribution and details of duty, the religious exercises, the ceremonials of the table, the fires, the lights, the watch, even the labours of the observatory and the notation of the tides and the sky,—nothing should be intermitted that had contributed to make up the day.

My next was to practise on the lessons we had learned from the Esquimaux. I had studied them carefully, and determined that their form of habitation and their peculiarities of diet, without their unthrift and filth, were the safest and best to which the necessity of our circumstances invited us.

My journal tells how these resolves were carried out:—

"*September* 6.—We are at it, all hands, sick and well, each man according to his measure, working at our winter's home. We are none of us in condition to brave the frost, and our fuel is nearly out.

"The sledge is to bring us moss and turf from wherever the men can scrape it. This is an excellent non-conductor; and when we get the quarter-deck well padded with it, we shall have a nearly cold-proof covering. Down below we will enclose a space some eighteen feet square, and pack it from floor to ceiling with inner walls of the same material. The floor itself we are calking carefully with plaster of Paris and common paste, and will cover it, when we have done, with Manilla oakum a couple of inches deep, and a canvas carpet. The entrance is to be from the hold, by a low, moss-lined tunnel, the *tossut* of the native huts, with as many doors and curtains to close it up as our ingenuity can devise. This is to be our apartment of all uses,—not a very large one; but we are only ten to stow away, and the closer the warmer.

"*September* 9.—All hands but the carpenter and Morton are again out 'mossing.'

"*September* 10.—'The work goes bravely on.' We have got moss enough for our roof, and something to spare for below. To-morrow we begin to strip off the outer-deck planking of the brig, and to stack it for firewood. It is cold work, hatches open and no fires going; but we saved time enough for our Sunday's exercises, though we forego its rest.

"I determined to try a novel expedient for catching seal. Not more than ten miles to seaward the icebergs keep up a rude stream of broken ice and water, and the seals resort there in scanty numbers to breathe. I drove out with my dogs, taking Hans along; but we found the spot so hemmed in by loose and fragile ice that there was no approaching it. The thermometer was 8°, and a light breeze increased my difficulties.

"*Deo volente*, I will be more lucky to-morrow. I am going to take my long Kentucky rifle, the kayack, an Esquimaux harpoon with its attached line and bladder, *naligeit* and *awahtok*, and a pair of large snow-shoes to boot. My plan this time is to kneel where the ice is unsafe, resting my weight on the broad surface of the snow-shoes, Hans following astride of his kayack, as a sort of life-preserver in case of breaking in. If I am fortunate enough to stalk within gun range, Hans will take to the water and secure the game before it sinks. We will be gone for some days probably, tenting it in the open air; but our sick men—that is to say, all of us—are languishing for fresh meat."

I started with Hans and five dogs, and in a couple of hours we emerged upon a plain unlimited to the eye and smooth as a billiard-table. Feathers of young frosting gave a plush-like nap to its surface, and toward the horizon dark columns of frost-smoke pointed clearly to the open water. This ice was firm enough; our experience satisfied us that it was not a very recent freezing. We pushed on without hesitation, cheering ourselves with the expectation of coming every minute to the seals. We passed a second ice-growth; it was not so strong as the one we had just come over, but still safe for a party like ours. On we went at a brisker gallop, maybe for another mile, when Hans sang out, at the top of his voice, "Pusey! puseymut! seal, seal!" At the same instant the dogs bounded forward, and, as I looked up, I saw crowds of grey netsik, the rough or hispid seal of the whalers, disporting in an open sea of water.

I had hardly welcomed the spectacle when I saw that we had passed upon a new belt of ice that was obviously unsafe. To turn was impossible; we had to keep up our gait. We urged on the dogs with whip and voice, the ice rolling like leather beneath the sledge-runners; it was more than a mile to the lump of solid ice. Fear gave to the poor beasts their utmost speed, and our voices were soon hushed to silence.

This desperate race against fate could not last: the rolling of the tough salt-water ice terrified our dogs; and when within fifty paces from the floe they paused. The left-hand runner went through; our leader "Toodlamick" followed, and in one second the entire left of the sledge was submerged. My first thought was to liberate the dogs. I leaned forward to cut poor Tood's traces, and the next minute was swimming in a little circle of pasty ice and water alongside him. Hans, dear good fellow, drew near to help me, uttering piteous expressions in broken English; but I ordered him to throw himself on his belly, with his hands and legs extended, and to make for the island by cogging himself forward with his jack-knife. In the meantime—a mere instant—I was floundering about with sledge, dogs, and lines, in confused puddle around me.

I succeeded in cutting poor Tood's lines and letting him scramble to the ice, for the poor fellow was drowning me with his piteous caresses, and made my way for the sledge; but I found that it would not buoy me, and that I had no resource but to try the circumference of the hole. Around this I paddled faithfully, the miserable ice always yielding when my hopes of a lodgment were greatest. During this process I enlarged my circle of operations to a very uncomfortable diameter, and was beginning to feel weaker after every effort. Hans meanwhile had reached the firm ice, and was on his knees, like a good Moravian, praying incoherently in English and Esquimax; at every fresh crushing-in of the ice he would ejaculate "God!" and when I recommenced my paddling he recommenced his prayers.

I was nearly gone. My knife had been lost in cutting out the dogs; and a spare one which I carried in my trousers-pocket was so enveloped in the wet skins that I could not reach it. I owed my extrication at last to a newly broken team dog, who was still fast to the sledge, and in struggling carried one of the runners choke against the edge of the circle. All my previous attempts to use the sledge as a bridge had failed, for it broke through, to the much greater injury of the ice. I felt that it was a last chance. I threw myself on my back, so as to lessen as much as possible my weight, and placed the nape of my neck against the rim or edge of the ice; then with caution slowly bent my leg, and, placing the ball of my mocassined foot against the sledge, I pressed steadily against the runner, listening to the half-yielding crunch of the ice beneath.

Presently I felt that my head was pillowed by the ice, and that my wet fur jumper was sliding up the surface. Next came my shoulders; they were fairly on. One more decided push, and I was launched up on the ice and safe. I reached the ice-floe, and was rubbed by Hans with frightful zeal. We saved all the dogs; but the sledge, kayack, tent, gun, snow-shoes, and everything besides, were left behind.

On reaching the ship, after a twelve-mile trot, I found so much of comfort and warm welcome that I forgot my failure. The fire was lit up, and one of our few birds slaughtered forthwith. It is with real gratitude that I look back upon my escape, and bless the great presiding Goodness for the very many resources which remain to us.

CHAPTER XIII.

NEGOTIATIONS WITH THE ESQUIMAUX.

I FIND that my journal is exceedingly meagre for the period of our anxious preparations to meet the winter, and that I have omitted to mention the course of circumstances which led us step by step into familiar communication with the Esquimaux.

My last notice of this strange people, whose fortunes became afterward so closely connected with our own, was at the time of Myouk's escape from imprisonment on board the brig. Although, during my absence on the attempted visit to Beechy Island, the men I had left behind had frequent and unrestrained intercourse with them, I myself saw no natives in Rensselaer Bay till immediately after the departure of Petersen and his companions. Just then, by a coincidence which convinced me how closely we had been under surveillance, a party of three made their appearance, as if to note for themselves our condition and resources.

When the three visitors came to us near the end of August, I established them in a tent below deck, with a copper lamp, a cooking-basin, and a liberal supply of slush for fuel. I left them under guard when I went to bed at two in the morning, contentedly eating and cooking and eating again, without the promise of an intermission. They repaid my liberality by stealing not only buffalo-robes, the lamp, boiler, and cooking-pot they had used for the feast, but Nannook also, my best dog. If the rest of my team had not been worn down by over-travel, no doubt they would have taken them all.

The theft of these articles embarrassed me. I was indisposed to take it as an act of hostility. Their pilferings before this had been conducted with such a superb simplicity, the detection followed by such honest explosions of laughter, that I could not help thinking they had some law of general appropriation, less removed from the Lycurgan than the Mosaic code. But it was plain, at least, that we were now too few to watch our property as we had done, and that our gentleness was to some extent misunderstood.

I was puzzled how to inflict punishment, but saw that I must act vigorously, even at a venture. I despatched my two best walkers, Morton and Riley, as soon as I heard of the theft of the stores, with orders to make all speed to Anoatok, and overtake the thieves, who, I thought, would probably halt there to rest. They found young Myouk making himself quite comfortable in the hut, in company with Sievu, the wife of Metek, and Aningna, the wife of Marsinga, and the buffalo-robes already tailored into kapetahs on their backs.

A continued search of the premises recovered the cooking-utensils, and a number of other things of greater or less value that we had not missed from the brig. With the prompt ceremonial which outraged law delights in among the officials of the police everywhere, the women were stripped and tied; and then, laden with their stolen goods and as much walrus-beef besides from their own stores as would pay for their board, they were marched on the instant back to the brig.

The thirty miles was a hard walk for them; but they did not complain, nor did their constabulary guardians, who had marched thirty miles already to apprehend them. It was hardly twenty-four hours since they left the brig with their booty before they were prisoners in the hold, with a dreadful white man for keeper, who never addressed to them a word that had not all the terrors of an unintelligible reproof, and whose scowl, I flatter myself, exhibited a well-arranged variety of menacing and demoniacal expressions.

They had not even the companionship of Myouk. Him

I had despatched to Metek, "head-man of Etah, and others," with the message of a melo-dramatic tyrant, to negotiate for their ransom. For five long days the women had to sigh and sing and cry in solitary converse,—their appetite continuing excellent, it should be remarked, though mourning the while a rightfully-impending doom. At last the great Metek arrived. He brought with him Ootuniah, another man of elevated social position, and quite a sledge-load of knives, tin cups, and other stolen goods, refuse of wood and scraps of iron, the sinful prizes of many covetings.

I may pass over our peace conferences and the indirect advantages which I, of course, derived from having the opposing powers represented in my own capital. But the splendours of our Arctic centre of civilisation, with its wonders of art and science,—our "fire-death" ordnance included,—could not all of them impress Metek so much as the intimations he had received of our superior physical endowments. Nomads as they are, these people know better than all the world besides what endurance and energy it requires to brave the moving ice and snow-drifts. Metek thought, no doubt, that our strength was gone with the withdrawing party; but the fact that, within ten hours after the loss of our buffalo-skins, we had marched to their hut, seized three of the culprits, and marched them back to the brig as prisoners,—such a sixty miles' achievement as this they thoroughly understood. It confirmed them in the faith that the whites are, and of right ought to be, everywhere the dominant tribe.

The protocol was arranged without difficulty, though not without the accustomed number of adjournments for festivity and repose. It abounded in protestations of power, fearlessness, and good-will by each of the contracting parties, which meant as much as such protestations usually do on both sides the Arctic circle. I could give a summary of it without invading the privacy of a diplomatic bureau, for I have notes of it that were taken by a subordinate; but I prefer passing at once to the reciprocal engagements in which it resulted.

On the part of the Esquimaux, they were after this fashion:—

"We promise that we will not steal. We promise we will bring you fresh meat. We promise we will sell or lend you dogs. We will keep you company whenever you want us, and show you where to find the game."

On the part of the white men, the stipulation was of this ample equivalent:—

"We promise that we will not visit you with death or sorcery, nor do you any hurt or mischief whatsoever. We will shoot for you on our hunts. You shall be made welcome aboard ship. We will give you presents of needles, pins, two kinds of knife, a hoop, three bits of hard wood, some fat, an awl, and some sewing-thread; and we will trade with you of these and everything else you want, for walrus and seal-meat of the first quality."

This treaty—which, though I have spoken of it jocosely, was really an affair of much interest to us—was ratified, with Hans and Morton as my accredited representatives, by a full assembly of the people at Etah. All our future intercourse was conducted under it. It was not solemnised by an oath, but it was never broken. We went to and fro between the villages and the brig, paid our visits of courtesy and necessity on both sides, met each other in hunting-parties on the floe and the ice-foot, organized a general community of interests, and really, I believe, established some personal attachments deserving of the name. As long as we remained prisoners of the ice, we were indebted to them for invaluable counsel in relation to our hunting expeditions; and in the joint hunt we shared alike, according to their own laws. Our dogs were in one sense common property; and often have they robbed themselves to offer supplies of food to our starving teams. They gave us supplies of meat at critical periods; we were able to do as much for them. They learned to look on us only as benefactors; and, I know, mourned our departure bitterly.

"*September* 17.—Writing by this miserable flicker of my pork-fat lamp, I can hardly steady pen, paper, or thought. All hands have rested after a heavy week's work, which has advanced us nobly in our arrangements for the winter. The season is by our tables at least three weeks earlier than the last, and everything indicates a severe ordeal ahead of us.

"Just as we were finishing our chapter this morning in the 'Book of Ruth,' M'Gary and Morton, who had been to Anoatok, came in triumphantly, pretty well worn down by their fifty miles' travel, but with good news, and a flipper of walrus that must weigh some forty pounds. Ohlsen and Hans are in too. They arrived as we were sitting down to celebrate the Anoatok ratification of our treaty of the 6th.

"It is a strange life we are leading. We are absolutely nomads, so far as there can be anything of pastoral life in this region; and our wild encounter with the elements seems to agree with us all. Our table-talk at supper was as merry as a marriage bell. One party was just in from a seventy-four miles' trip with the dogs; another from a foot journey of a hundred and sixty, with five nights on the floe. Each had his story to tell.

"*September* 20.—The natives are really acting up to contract. They are on board to-day, and I have been off with a party of them on a hunt inland. We had no great luck; the weather was against us, and there are signs of a gale."

My next extracts show the progress of our winter arrangements.

"*September* 30.—We have been clearing up on the ice.

"Thanks to our allies the Esquimaux, our beef-house is now a pile of barrels holding our water-soaked beef and pork. Flour, beans, and dried apples make a quadrangular blockhouse on the floe; from one corner of it rises our flagstaff, lighting up the dusky grey with its red and white ensign, only on Sunday giving place to the Henry Grinnell flag, of happy memories.

"From this, along an avenue that opens abeam of the brig,—New London Avenue, named after M'Gary's town at home,—are our boats and square cordage. Outside of all these is a magnificent hut of barrel-frames and snow, to accommodate our Esquimaux visitors—the only thing about it exposed to hazard being the tempting woodwork. What remains to complete our camp-plot is the rope barrier that is to mark out our little curtilage around the vessel; this, when finished, is to be the dividing-line between us and the rest of mankind.

"There is something in the simplicity of all this *simplex munditiis*, which might commend itself to the most rigorous taste. Nothing is wasted on ornament.

"*October* 4.—I sent Hans and Hickey two days ago out to the hunting-ice, to see if the natives have had any luck with the walrus. They are back to-night with bad news, —no meat, no Esquimaux. These strange children of the snow have made a mysterious flitting—where or how it is hard to guess, for they have no sledges. They cannot have travelled very far; and yet they have such unquiet impulses, that, once on the track, no civilised man can say where they will bring up.

"Ohlsen had just completed a sledge, fashioned like the Smith Sound *kommetik*, with an improved curvature of the runners. It weighs only twenty-four pounds, and, though I think it too short for light draught, it is just the article our Etah neighbours would delight in for their land-portages. I intended it for them, as a great price for a great stock of walrus-meat; but the other parties to the bargain have flown.

"*October 5.*—We are nearly out of fresh meat again, one rabbit and three ducks being our sum total. We have been on short allowance for several days. What vegetables we have—the dried apples and peaches, and pickled cabbage — have lost much of their anti-scorbutic virtue by constant use. Our spices are all gone. Except four small bottles of horse-radish, our *carte* is comprised in three lines—bread, beef, pork.

"I must be off after these Esquimaux. They certainly have meat, and wherever they have gone we can follow. Once upon their trail, our hungry instincts will not risk being baffled. I will stay only long enough to complete my latest root-beer brewage. Its basis is the big crawling willow, the miniature giant of our Arctic forests, of which we laid in a stock some weeks ago. It is quite pleasantly bitter, and I hope to get it fermenting in the deck-house without extra fuel, by heat from below.

"*October 7.*—Lively sensation, as they say in the land of olives and champagne. 'Nannook, nannook!'—'A bear, a bear!'—Hans and Morton in a breath!

"To the scandal of our domestic regulations, the guns were all impracticable. While the men were loading and capping anew, I seized my pillow-companion six shooter, and ran on deck. A medium-sized bear, with a four months' cub, was in active warfare with our dogs. They were hanging on her skirts, and she with wonderful alertness was picking out one victim after another, snatching him by the nape of the neck, and flinging him many feet, or rather yards, by a barely perceptible movement of her head.

"I lodged a pistol-ball in the side of the cub. Ohlsen wounded the mother as she went, but she scarcely noticed it. She tore down, by single efforts of her forearms, the barrels of frozen beef which made the triple walls of the storehouse, mounted the rubbish, and snatching up a half barrel of herrings, carried it down by her teeth, and was making off. It was time to close, I thought. Going up within half-pistol range, I gave her six buckshot. She dropped, but instantly rose, and, getting her cub into its former position, moved off once more.

"This time she would really have escaped but for the admirable tactics of our new recruits from the Esquimaux. The dogs of Smith's Sound are educated more thoroughly than any of their southern brethren. Next to the walrus, the bear is the staple of diet to the north, and except the fox, supplies the most important element of the wardrobe. Unlike the dogs we had brought with us from Baffin's Bay, these were trained, not to attack, but to embarrass. They ran in circles round the bear, and when pursued would keep ahead with regulated gait, their comrades effecting a diversion at the critical moment by a nip at her hind-quarters. This was done so systematically, and with so little seeming excitement, as to strike every one on board. I have seen bear-dogs elsewhere that had been drilled to relieve each other in the *melée* and avoid the direct assault· but here, two dogs without even a demonstration of attack, would put themselves before the path of the animal, and retreating right and left, lead him into a profitless pursuit that checked his advance completely.

"The poor animal was still backing out, yet still fighting, carrying along her wounded cub, embarrassed by the dogs, yet gaining distance from the brig, when Hans and myself threw in the odds in the shape of a couple of rifle-balls. She staggered in front of her young one, faced us in death-like defiance, and only sank when pierced by six more bullets.

"The little cub sprang upon the corpse of her mother, and raised a woeful lamentation over her wounds. She repelled my efforts to noose her with great ferocity; but at last, completely muzzled with a line fastened by a running knot between her jaws and the back of her head, she moved off to the brig amid the clamour of the dogs. We have her now chained alongside, but snarling and snapping constantly, evidently suffering from her wound.

"*October* 8.—When I was out in the *Advance*, with Captain de Haven, I satisfied myself that it was a vulgar prejudice to regard the liver of the bear as poisonous. I ate of it freely myself, and succeeded in making it a favourite dish with the mess. But I find to my cost that it may sometimes be more savoury than safe. The cub's liver was my supper last night, and to-day I have the symptoms of poison in full measure—vertigo, diarrhœa, and their concomitants.

"*October* 10.—If I was asked what, after darkness and cold and scurvy, are the three besetting curses of our Arctic sojourn, I should say, RATS, RATS, RATS. A mother-rat bit my finger to the bone last Friday, as I was intruding my hand into a bear-skin mitten which she had chosen as a homestead for her little family. I withdrew it of course with instinctive courtesy; but among them they carried off the mitten before I could suck the finger.

"Last week I sent down Rhina, the most intelligent dog of our whole pack, to bivouac in their citadel forward; I thought she might at least be able to defend herself against them, for she had distinguished herself in the bear-hunt. She slept very well for a couple of hours on a bed she had chosen for herself on the top of some iron spikes. But the rats could not or would not forgo the horny skin about her paws; and they gnawed her feet and nails so ferociously, that we drew her up yelping and vanquished.

"*October* 13.—The Esquimaux have not been near us, and it is a puzzle of some interest where they have retreated to. Wherever they are, there must be our hunting-grounds, for they certainly have not changed their quarters to a more destitute region. I have sent Morton and Hans to-day to track them out if they can. They carry a hand-sledge with them, Ohlsen's last manufacture, ride with the dog-sledge as far as Anoatok, and leave the old dogs of our team there. From that point they are to try a device of my own. We have a couple of dogs that we got from these same Esquimaux, who are at least as instinctive as their former masters. One of these they are to let run, holding the other by a long leash. I feel confident that the free dog will find the camping-ground, and I think it probable the other will follow. I thought of tying the two together; but it would embarrass their movements, and give them something to occupy their minds, besides the leading object of their mission.

"*October* 14.—Wilson and Hickey reported last night a wolf at the meat-house. Now, the meat-house is a thing of too much worth to be left to casualty, and a wolf might incidentally add some freshness of flavour to its contents.

So I went out in all haste with the Marston rifle, but without my mittens, and with only a single cartridge. The metal burnt my hands, as metal is apt to do at 50° below the point of freezing; but I got a somewhat rapid shot. I hit one of our dogs, a truant from Morton's team; luckily a flesh wound only, for he is too good a beast to lose. I could have sworn he was a wolf.

"*October* 19.—Our black dog Erebus has come back to the brig. Morton has perhaps released him, but he has more probably broken loose.

"*October* 21.—Hard at it still, slinging chains and planting shores. The thermometer is too near zero for work like this. We swaddle our feet in old cloth, and guard our hands with fur mits; but the cold iron bites through them all.

"6.30 P.M.—Morton and Hans are in, after tracking the Esquimaux to the lower settlement of Etah. I cannot give their report to-night: the poor fellows are completely knocked up by the hardships of their march. Hans, who is always careless of powder and fire-arms,—a trait which I have observed among both the American and the Oriental savages,—exploded his powder-flask while attempting to kindle a tinder fire. The explosion has risked his hand. I have dressed it, extracting several pieces of foreign matter, and poulticing it in yeast and charcoal. Morton has frostbitten both his heels; I hope not too severely, for the indurated skin of the heel makes it a bad region for suppuration. But they bring us two hundred and seventy pounds of walrus-meat, and a couple of foxes. This supply, with what we have remaining of our two bears, must last us till the return of daylight allows us to join the natives in their hunts.

"The light is fast leaving us. The sun has ceased to

reach the vessel. The north-eastern headlands, or their southern faces up the fiords, have still a warm yellow tint, and the pinnacles of the icebergs far out on the floes are lighted up at noonday; but all else is dark shadow."

CHAPTER XIV.

THE ESQUIMAUX VILLAGE—A WALRUS HUNT.

Morton reached the huts beyond Anoatok upon the fourth day after leaving the brig.

There were four of them, but two of them are in ruins. They were all of them the homes of families only four winters ago. Of the two which are still habitable, Myouk, his father, mother, brother and sister occupied one; and Awahtok and Ootuniah, with their wives and three young ones, the other. The little community had lost two of its members by death since the spring.

They received Morton and his companions with much kindness, giving them water to drink, rubbing their feet, drying their moccasins, and the like. The women, who did this, with something of the goodwife's air of prerogative, seemed to have toned down much of the rudeness which characterised the bachelor settlement at Anoatok. The lamps were cheerful and smokeless, and the huts much less filthy. Each had its two lamps constantly burning, with a framework of bone-hooks and walrus-line above them for drying the wet clothes of the household. Except a few dog-skins, which are used as a support to the small of the back, the dais was destitute of sleeping accommodations altogether: a single walrus-hide was spread out for Morton and Hans. The hut had the usual *tossut*, or entrance passage, at least twelve feet long—very low, straight, and level, until it reached the inner part of the chamber, when it rose abruptly by a small hole, through which with some squeezing was the entrance into the true apartment. Over this entrance was the rude window, with its scraped seal-intestine instead of glass, heavily coated with frost of course ; but a small eye-hole commanding the bay enabled the indwellers to peep out and speak or call to any who were outside. A smoke-hole passed through the roof.

When all the family, with Morton and Hans, were gathered together, the two lamps in full blaze, and the narrow hole of entrance covered by a flat stone, the heat became insupportable. Outside, the thermometer stood at 30° below zero; within, 90° above; a difference of 120°.

The vermin were not as troublesome as in the Anoatok dormitory, the natives hanging their clothing over the lamp-frames, and lying down to sleep perfectly naked, with the exception of a sort of T bandage, as surgeons call it, of seal-skin, three inches wide, worn by the women as a badge of their sex, and supported by a mere strip around the hips.

After sharing the supper of their hosts, the visitors stretched themselves out and passed the night in unbroken perspiration and slumber. It was evident from the meagreness of the larder that the hunters of the family had work to do; and from some signs, which did not escape the sagacity of Morton, it was plain that Myouk and his father had determined to seek their next dinner upon the floes. They were going upon a walrus hunt; and Morton, true to the mission with which I had charged him invited himself and Hans to be of the party.

I have not yet described one of these exciting incidents of Esquimaux life. Morton was full of the one he witnessed; and his account of it when he came back was so graphic, that I shall be glad to escape from the egotism of personal narrative by giving it in his own words.

The party which he attended upon their walrus hunt had three sledges. One was to be taken to a *cache* in the neighbourhood; the other two dragged at a quick run toward the open water, about ten miles off to the south-west. They had but nine dogs to these two sledges, one man only riding, the others running by turns. As they neared the new ice, and where the black wastes of mingled cloud and water betokened the open sea, they would from time to time remove their hoods and listen intently for the animal's voice.

After a while Myouk became convinced, from signs or sounds, or both,—for they were inappreciable by Morton,—that the walrus were waiting for him in a small space of recently-open water that was glazed over with a few days' growth of ice; and moving gently on, they soon heard its characteristic bellow. The walrus, like some of the higher order of beings to which he has been compared, is fond of his own music, and will lie for hours listening to himself. His vocalisation is something between the mooing of a cow and the deepest baying of a mastiff: very round and full, with its barks or detached notes repeated rather quickly seven to nine times in succession.

The party now formed in single file, following in each other's steps, and, guided by an admirable knowledge of ice-topography, wound behind hummocks and ridges in a serpentine approach toward a group of pond-like discolourations, recently-frozen ice-spots, but surrounded by firmer and older ice.

When within half a mile of these, the line broke, and each man crawled toward a separate pool—Morton on his hands and knees following Myouk. In a few minutes the walrus were in sight. They were five in number, rising at intervals through the ice in a body, and breaking it up with an explosive puff that might have been heard for miles. Two large grim-looking males were conspicuous as the leaders of the group.

Now for the marvel of the craft. When the walrus is above water, the hunter is flat and motionless; as he begins to sink, alert and ready for a spring. The animal's head is hardly below the water-line before every man is in a rapid run; and again, as if by instinct, before the beast returns, all are motionless behind protecting knolls of ice. They seem to know beforehand not only the time he will be absent, but the very spot at which he will re-appear. In this way, hiding and advancing by turns, Myouk, with Morton at his heels, has reached a plate of thin ice, hardly strong enough to bear them, at the very brink of the water-pool the walrus are curvetting in.

Myouk, till now phlegmatic, seems to waken with excitement. His coil of walrus-hide, a well-trimmed line of many fathoms' length, is lying at his side. He fixes one end of it in an iron barb, and fastens this loosely by a socket upon a shaft of unicorn's horn; the other end is already looped, or, as sailors would say, "doubled in a bight." It is the work of a moment. He has grasped the harpoon; the water is in motion. Puffing with pent-up respiration, the walrus is within a couple of fathoms close before him. Myouk rises slowly—his right arm thrown back, the left flat at his side. The walrus looks about him, shaking the water from his crest; Myouk throws up his left arm, and the animal, rising breast high, fixes one look before he plunges. It has cost him all that curiosity can cost; the harpoon is buried under his left flipper.

Though the walrus is down in a moment, Myouk is running at desperate speed from the scene of his victory, paying off his coil freely, but clutching the end by its loop. He seizes as he runs a small stick of bone, rudely pointed with iron, and by a sudden movement drives it into the ice; to this he secures his line, pressing it down close to the ice-surface with his feet.

Now comes the struggle. The hole is dashed in mad commotion with the struggles of the wounded beast; the line is drawn tight at one moment, the next relaxed: the hunter has not left his station. There is a crash of the ice; and rearing up through it are two walruses, not many yards from where he stands. One of them, the male, is excited and seemingly terrified; the other, the female, collected and vengeful. Down they go again, after one grim survey of the field; and on the instant Myouk has changed his position, carrying his coil with him and fixing it anew.

He has hardly fixed it before the pair have again risen, breaking up an area of ten feet diameter about the very spot he left. As they sink once more he again changes his place. And so the conflict goes on between address and force, till the victim, half exhausted, receives a second wound, and is played like a trout by the angler's reel.

Some idea may be formed of the ferocity of the walrus, from the fact that the battle which Morton witnessed, not without sharing some of its danger, lasted four hours—during which the animal rushed continually at the Esquimaux as they approached, tearing off great tables of ice with his tusks, and showing no indications of fear whatever. He received upward of seventy lance-wounds,—

Morton counted over sixty; and even then he remained hooked by his tusks to the margin of the ice, unable or unwilling to retire. His female fought in the same manner, but fled on receiving a lance-wound.

The Esquimaux seemed to be fully aware of the danger of venturing too near; for at the first onset of the walrus they jumped back far enough to be clear of the broken ice. Morton described the last three hours as wearing, on both sides, the aspect of an unbroken and seemingly doubtful combat.

The method of landing the beast upon the ice, too, showed a great deal of clever contrivance. They made two pair of incisions in the neck, where the hide is very thick, about six inches apart and parallel to each other, so as to form a couple of bands. A line of cut hide, about a quarter of an inch in diameter, was passed under one of these bands and carried up on the ice to a firm stick well secured in the floe, where it went through a loop, and was then taken back to the animal, made to pass under the second band, and led off to the Esquimaux. This formed a sort of "double purchase," the blubber so lubricating the cord as to admit of a free movement. By this contrivance the beast, weighing some seven hundred pounds, was hauled up and butchered at leisure.

The two sledges now journeyed homeward, carrying the more valued parts of their prize. The intestines and a large share of the carcass were buried up in the cavities of a berg; Lucullus himself could not have dreamed of a grander icehouse.

As they doubled the little island which stood in front of their settlement, the women ran down the rocks to meet them. A long hail carried the good news; and, as the party alighted on the beach, knives were quickly at work, the allotment of the meat being determined by well-understood hunter laws. The Esquimaux, however gluttonously they may eat, evidently bear hunger with as little difficulty as excess. None of the morning party had breakfasted; yet it was after ten o'clock at night before they sat down to dinner. "Sat down to dinner!" This is the only expression of our own gastrology which is applicable to an Esquimaux feast. They truly sit down, man, woman, and child, knife in hand, squatting cross-legged around a formidable joint,—say forty pounds,—falling to like college commoners after grace. I have seen many such feeds. Han's account, however, of the glutton-festival is too characteristic to be omitted :—

"Why, Cappen Ken, sir, even the children ate all night; you know the little two-year-old that Awiu carried in her hood—the one that bit you when you tickled it? Yes. Well, Cappen Ken, sir, that baby cut for herself, with a knife made out of an iron hoop, and so heavy that it could barely lift it, and cut and ate, and ate and cut, as long as I looked at it."

"Well, Hans, try now and think; for I want an accurate answer: how much as to weight or quantity would you say that child ate?" Hans is an exact and truthful man: he pondered a little and said that he could not answer my question. "But I know this, sir, that it ate a *sipak*"—the Esquimaux name for the lump which is cut off close to the lips—"as large as its own head; and three hours afterward, when I went to bed, it was cutting off another lump and eating still." A sipak, like the Dutch governor's foot, is, however, a varying unit of weight.

CHAPTER XV.

THE COMING WINTER.

"*October* 26.—The thermometer at 34° below zero, but fortunately no wind blowing. We go on with the out-door work. We burn but seventy pounds of fuel a day, most of it in the galley—the fire being allowed to go out between meals. We go without fire altogether for four hours of the night; yet such is the excellence of our moss-walls and the air-proof of our *tossut*, that, when our housing is arranged, and the main hatch secured with a proper weather-tight screen of canvas, we shall be able, I hope, to meet the extreme cold of February and March without fear.

"Darkness is the worst enemy we have to face; but we will strive against the scurvy in spite of him, till the light days of sun and vegetation.

"Wilson and Brooks are my principal subjects of anxiety; for although Morton and Hans are on their backs, making four of our ten, I can see strength of system in their cheerfulness of heart. The best prophylactic is a hopeful, sanguine temperament; the best cure, moral resistance—that spirit of combat against every trial, which is alone true bravery.

"*October* 27.—The work is going on; we are ripping off the extra planking of our deck for fuel during the winter. The cold increases fast, and in spite of all my efforts we will have to burn largely into the brig. I prepared for this two months ago, and satisfied myself, after a consultation with the carpenter, that we may cut away some seven or eight tons of fuel without absolutely destroying her sea-worthiness."

My narrative has now reached a period at which everything like progress was suspended. The increasing cold and brightening stars,—the labours, anxieties, and sickness that pressed upon us,—these almost engross the pages of my journal. Now and then I find some marvel such as Petersen's about the fox's dexterity as a hunter; Hans tells me of domestic life in South Greenland, or of a seal-hunt and a wrecked kayack; or perhaps M'Gary repeats his thrice-told tale of humour; but the night has closed down upon us, and we are hibernating through it.

Yet some of these are topics of interest. The intense beauty of the Arctic firmament can hardly be imagined. It looks close above our heads, with its stars magnified in glory, and the very planets twinkling so much as to baffle the observations of our astronomer. I am afraid to speak of some of these night-scenes. I have trodden the deck and the floes, when the life of earth seemed suspended,—its movements, its sounds, its colouring, its companionships; and as I looked on the radiant hemisphere, circling above me as if rendering worship to the unseen centre of light, I have ejaculated in humility of spirit, "Lord, what is man that Thou art mindful of him?" And then I have thought of the kindly world we had left, with its revolving sunshine and shadow, and the other stars that gladden it in their changes, and the hearts that warmed to us there, till I lost myself in memories of those who are not—and they bore me back to the stars again.

The narration of one day's hopes and fears, troubles, privations, and trials,—I am sorry I cannot add triumphs,

—so much resembles that of the next, that I feel it would be but tiring the patience of the reader were I to detail, with the same degree of minuteness which I have hitherto done, the daily progress of our little party, and the great cause in which we are engaged.

The winter is now upon us, and little or nothing can be done either to effect the liberation of the brig from her icy fetters, or to further our explorations.

On board the brig the mode of life is the same as last winter, except that we are subject to greater privations, consequent on the great demands which have been made upon the stores. We have little to amuse ourselves, and we go through the monotonous round of the day's duties with as much celerity and ready will, as our drooping circumstances will admit of.

I cannot hide from myself the fact that the main object of our expedition must now be finally abandoned; and our duty, in the next instance, is toward ourselves: to wait the return of light in order to accomplish our escape from the ice,—with the brig if possible, if impossible, without it,—before the frail appliances and stores which are now left are entirely exhausted. Of course, it would be both impolitic and unwise to apprise the crew of my thoughts on this painful subject, so I will keep my own counsel in the meantime. I can see, however, that I am not alone in my convictions.

During November, I observed a few of my best men getting nervous and depressed—M'Gary paced the deck all one Sunday in a fit of home-sickness, without eating a meal—I do my best to cheer them; but it is hard work to hide one's own trials for the sake of others who have not as many. I am glad of my professional drill and its companion influence over the sick and toil-worn. I could not get along at all unless I combined the offices of physician and commander. You cannot punish sick men.

December saw the brig fitted up for the winter; and, all things considered, very comfortably we made it. Tom Hickey, our good-humoured, blundering cabin-boy, decorated since poor Schubert's death with the dignities of cook, is in that little dirty cot on the starboard-side; the rest are bedded in rows, Mr Brooks and myself choke aft. Our bunks are close against the frozen moss-wall, where we can take in the entire family at a glance. The apartment measures twenty feet by eighteen; its height six feet four inches at one place, but diversified elsewhere by beams crossing at different distances from the floor. The avenue by which it is approached is barely to be seen in the moss-wall forward. The avenue—Ben-Djerback is our poetic name for it—closes on the inside with a door well patched with flannel, from which, stooping upon all-fours, you back down a descent of four feet in twelve, through a tunnel three feet high and two feet six inches broad. It would have been a tight squeeze for a man like Mr Brooks, when he was better fed and fatter. Arrived at the bottom, you straighten yourself, and a second door admits you into the dark and sorrowing hold, empty of stores, and stripped to its naked ceiling for firewood. From this we grope our way to the main hatch, and mount by a rude stairway of boxes into the open air.

"*December* 2.—Many of the men are down with sickness and scurvy, and this adds greatly to my anxiety. M'Gary, Riley, Wilson, and Brooks, are all on the sick-list, and as for poor Morton, I am afraid I will lose him. Poor fellows, I can ill afford to lose any of them; but if Morton dies, it will be a great loss indeed. He is not only one of my most intelligent men, but he is daring, cool, and every way trustworthy.

"On the 7th we had an agreeable surprise. I was asleep in the forenoon, after the fatigue of an extra night-watch, when I was called to the deck by the report of 'Esquimaux sledges.' They came on rapidly, five sledges, with teams of six dogs each, most of the drivers strangers to us; and in a few minutes were at the brig. Their errand was of charity: they were bringing back to us Bonsall and Petersen, two of the party that left us on the 28th of August.

"The party had many adventures and much suffering to tell of. They had verified by painful and perilous experience all I had anticipated for them. But the most stirring of their announcements was the condition they had left their associates in, two hundred miles off, divided in their counsels, their energies broken, and their provisions nearly gone. Space and opportunity will not permit of my giving an account of their wanderings and privations, but they were very severe. My first thought was of the means of rescuing them. After a little necessary delay I despatched a party to relieve them.

"On the morning of the 12th Brooks awoke me with the cry of 'Esquimaux again!' I dressed hastily, and groping my way over the pile of boxes that leads up from the hold into the darkness above, made out a group of human figures, masked by the hooded jumpers of the natives. They stopped at the gangway, and, as I was about to challenge, one of them sprang forward and grasped my hand. It was Doctor Hayes. A few words, dictated by suffering, certainly not by any anxiety as to his reception, and at his bidding the whole party came upon deck. Poor fellows! I could only grasp their hands and give them a brother's welcome.

"One by one they all came in and were housed. Poor fellows! as they threw open their Esquimaux garments by the stove, how they relished the scanty luxuries which we had to offer them! The coffee and the meat-biscuit soup, and the molasses and wheat bread, even the salt pork which our scurvy forbade the rest of us to touch,—how they relished it all! For more than two months they had lived on frozen seal and walrus-meat.

"*December* 23.—A very serious occurrence took place to-day, which might have resulted in disastrous consequences. A watch had been stationed in charge of the lamp, with the usual order of ' No uncovered lights.' He deserted his post. Soon afterward Hans found the cooking-room on fire. It was a horrible crisis; for no less than eight of our party were absolutely nailed to their beds, and there was nothing but a bulkhead between them and the fire. I gave short but instant orders, stationing a line between the tide-hole and the main hatch, detailing two men to work with me, and ordering all the rest who could move to their quarters. Dr Hayes with his maimed foot, Mr Brooks with his contracted legs, and poor Morton, otherwise among our best men, could do nothing.

"Before we reached the fire the entire bulkhead was in a blaze as well as the dry timbers and skin of the brig. Our moss walls, with their own tinder-like material and their light casing of inflammable wood, were entirely hidden by the flames. Fortunately the furs of the recently-returned party were at hand, and with them I succeeded in smothering the fire. But I was obliged to push through the blaze of our sailcloth bulkhead in order to defend the wall; and in my anxiety to save time, I had left the cabin without either cap or mittens. I got through somehow or other, and tore down the canvas which hung against that dangerous locality. Our rifles were in this corner, and their muzzles pointing in all directions.

"The water now began to pass down; but with the discharge of the first bucketful the smoke overcame me. As I found myself going I pushed for the hatchway, knowing that the bucket-line would *feel* me. Seeing was impossible; but, striking Ohlsen's legs as I fell, I was passed up to the deck, *minus* beard, eyebrows, and forelock, *plus* two burns on the forehead and one on each palm.

"In about three minutes after making way with the canvas the fire was got under, and in less than half an hour all was safe again. But the transition, for even the shortest time, from the fiery Shadrachin furnace-temperature below, to 46° below zero above, was intolerably trying. Every man suffered, and few escaped without frost-bitten fingers.

"The remembrance of the danger and its horrible results almost miraculously averted, shocks us all. Had we lost our brig, not a man could have survived. Without shelter, clothing, or food, what help could we have on the open ice field?

"*December 25, Christmas Day.*—All together again, the returned and the steadfast, we sat down to our Christmas dinner. There was more love than with the 'stalled ox' of former times; but of herbs none. We forgot our discomforts in the blessings which adhered to us still; and when we thought of the long road ahead of us, we thought of it hopefully. I pledged myself to give them their next Christmas with their homes; and each of us drank his 'absent friends' with ferocious zest over one-eighteenth part of a bottle of sillery,—the last of its hamper."

We entered upon the New-Year 1854 with mingled feelings of hope and dismay. The long, dull, dreary months of January and February "dragged their slow length along" without much variety or incidents worth noting. We devised plans by which we hoped to be able to get away from our frozen fortress, but could do nothing in the way of execution until the much-longed-for light re-appeared.

"*February* 10.—At length we have prognostications of the return of the blessed sun. The day is beginning to glow with its rays. The south at noon has almost an orange tinge. In ten days his direct rays will reach our hill tops, and in a week after he will be dispensing his blessed medicine among our sufferers."

It is hardly worth while to inflict on the reader a succession of journal-records like these. They tell of nothing but the varying symptoms of sick men, dreary, profitless hunts, relieved now and then by the signalised incident of a killed rabbit or a deer seen, and the longed-for advent of the solar light.

We worked on board—those of us who could work at all—at arranging a new gangway with a more gentle slope, to let some of the party crawl up from their hospital into the air. We were six, all told, out of eighteen, who could affect to hunt, cook, or nurse.

For myself, my thoughts had occupation enough in the question of our closing labours. I never lost my hope. I looked to the coming spring as full of responsibilities; but I had bodily strength and moral tone enough to look through them to the end. A trust, based on experience as well as on promises, buoyed me up at the worst of times. Call it fatalism, as you ignorantly may, there is that in the story of every eventful life which teaches the inefficiency of human means and the present control of a Supreme Agency. See how often relief has come at the moment of extremity, in forms strangely unsought, almost at the time unwelcome; see, still more, how the back has been strengthened to its increasing burden, and the heart cheered by some conscious influence of an unseen Power.

"*February* 21.—To-day the crests of the north-east headland were gilded by true sunshine, and all who were able assembled on deck to greet it. For the past ten days we have been watching the growing warmth of our landscape, as it emerged from buried shadow, through all the stages of distinctness of an India-ink washing, step by step, into the sharp, bold definition of our desolate harbour scene. We have marked every dash of colour which the great Painter in his benevolence vouchsafed to us; and now the empurpled blues, clear, unmistakable, the spreading lake, the flickering yellow; peering at all these, poor wretches! everything seemed superlative lustre and unsurpassable glory. We had so grovelled in darkness that we oversaw the light."

My journal for March is little else than a chronicle of sufferings. Our little party was quite broken down. Every man on board was tainted with scurvy, and it was not common to find more than three who could assist in caring for the rest. The greater number were in their bunks, absolutely unable to stir.

The circumstances were well fitted to bring out the character of individuals. Some were intensely grateful for every little act of kindness from their more fortunate messmates; some querulous; others desponding; others again wanted only strength to become mutinous. Brooks, my first officer, as stalwart a man-o'-war's man as ever faced an enemy, burst into tears when he first saw himself in the glass. On Sunday, the 4th, our last remnant of fresh meat had been doled out. Our invalids began to sink rapidly. The region about our harbour ceased to furnish its scanty contingent of game. One of our huntsmen,

Petersen, never very reliable in anything, declared himself unfit for further duty. Hans was unsuccessful: he made several wide circuits, and saw deer twice; but once they were beyond range, and the next time his rifle missed fire.

I tried the hunt for a long morning myself, without meeting a single thing of life, and was convinced, by the appearance of things on my return to the brig, that I should peril the *morale*, and with it the only hope, of my command by repeating the experiment.

I laboured, of course, with all the ingenuity of a well-taxed mind, to keep up the spirits of my comrades. I cooked for them all imaginable compounds of our unvaried diet-list, and brewed up flax-seed and lime-juice and quinine and willow-stems into an abomination which was dignified as beer, and which some were persuaded for the time to believe such. But it was becoming more and more certain every hour, that unless we could renew our supplies of fresh meat, the days of the party were numbered.

I spare myself, as well as the readers of this hastily-compiled volume, when I pass summarily over the details of our condition at this time.

I look back at it with recollections like those of a nightmare. Yet I was borne up wonderfully. I never doubted for an instant that the same Providence which had guarded us through the long darkness of winter was still watching over us for good, and that it was yet in reserve for us—for some, I dared not hope for all—to bear back the tidings of our rescue to a Christian land. But how I did not see.

The advent of April brings with it a better state of matters. Petersen has so far recovered that he is able to go hunting, and he has met with some success; and never was blessing more welcome than the fresh meat with which his gun supplied our long starved table. Several of the crew are on their legs again, and things generally begin to assume a healthier aspect. Business, as far as our shattered constitutions will permit, is now the order of the day.

"*April* 20.—A relief-watch, of Riley, Morton, and Bonsall, are preparing to saw out sledge runners from the cross-beams of the brig. It is slow work. They are very weak, and the thermometer sinks at night to —26°. Nearly all our beams have been used up for fuel; but I have saved enough to construct two sledges. I want a sledge sufficiently long to bring the weight of the whale-boat and her stowage within the line of the runner; this will prevent her rocking and pitching when crossing hummocked ice, and enable us to cradle her firmly to the sledge.

"*April* 21.—Morton's heel is nearly closed, and there is apparently a sound bone underneath. He has been upon his back since October. I can now set this faithful and valuable man to active duty very soon.

"The beam was too long to be carried through our hatches; we therefore have sawed it as it stands, and will carry up the slabs separately. These slabs are but one and a half inch wide, and must be strengthened by iron bolts and cross-pieces; still they are all that we have. I made the bolts out of our cabin curtain-rods, long disused. Mr Petersen aids Ohlsen in grinding his tools. They will complete the job to-morrow,—for we must work on Sunday now,—and by Monday be able to begin at other things. Petersen undertakes to manufacture our cooking and mess-gear. I have a sad-looking assortment of battered rusty tins to offer him; but with the stove-pipe much may be done.

"*April* 22.—Gave rest for all but the sawyers, who keep manfully at the beam. Some notion of our weakness may be formed from the fact of these five poor fellows averaging among them but one foot per hour."

CHAPTER XVI.

PREPARATIONS FOR LEAVING THE BRIG.

We continued toiling on with our complicated preparations till the evening of the 24th, when Hans came back well laden with walrus meat. Three of the Esquimaux accompanied him, each with his sledge and dog-team fully equipped for a hunt. The leader of the party, Kalutunah, was a noble savage, greatly superior in everything to the others of his race. He greeted me with respectful courtesy, yet as one who might rightfully expect an equal measure of it in return, and, after a short interchange of salutations, seated himself in the post of honour at my side.

I waited, of course, till the company had fed and slept, for among savages especially haste is indecorous, and then, after distributing a few presents, opened to them my project of a northern exploration. Kalutunah received his knife and needles with a "Kuyanaka," "I thank you:" the first thanks I have heard from a native of this upper region. He called me his friend,—"Asakaoteet," "I love you well,"—and would be happy, he said, to join the "nalegak-soak" in a hunt.

The project was one that had engaged my thoughts long before daylight had renewed the possibility of carrying it out. I felt that the further shores beyond Kennedy Channel were still to be searched before our work could be considered finished; but we were without dogs, the indispensable means of travel. We had only four left out of sixty-two. Famine among the Esquimaux had been as disastrous as disease with us: they had killed all but thirty, and of these there were now sixteen picketed on the ice about the brig. The aid and influence of Kalutunah could secure my closing expedition.

I succeeded in making my arrangements with him, provisionally at least, and the morning after we all set out. The party consisted of Kalutunah, Shanghu, and Tatterat, an outlandish Esquimaux, who had his name from the Kitty-wake Gull, with their three sledges. Hans, armed with the Marston rifle, was my only companion from the ship's company. The natives carried no arms but the long knife and their unicorn ivory lances. Our whole equipment was by no means cumbersome: except the clothes upon our back and raw walrus-meat, we carried nothing.

We started with a wild yell of dogs and men in chorus, Kalutunah and myself leading. In about two hours we had reached a high berg about fifteen miles north of the brig. Here I reconnoitred the ice ahead. It was not cheering: the outside tide-channel, where I had broken through the fall before, was now full of squeezed ice, and the plain beyond the bergs seem much distorted. The Esquimaux, nevertheless, acceded to my wish to attempt the passage, and we were soon among the hummocks. We ran beside our sledges, clinging to the upstanders, but making, perhaps, four miles an hour where, unassisted by the dogs, we could certainly have made but one. Things began to look more auspicious.

We halted for lunch about thirty miles north of the brig, after having edged along the coast about thirty miles to the eastward. Lunch over, the journey began again, and we should have accomplished my wishes had it not been for the untoward influence of sundry bears. The tracks of these animals were becoming more and more numerous as we rounded one iceberg after another; and

L

we could see the beds they had worn in the snow while watching for seal. These swayed the dogs from their course: yet we kept edging onwards; and when in sight of the northern coast, about thirty miles from the central peak of the "Three Brothers," I saw a deep band of stratus lying over the horizon in the direction of Kennedy Channel. This water-sky indicated the continued opening of the channel, and made me more deeply anxious to proceed. But at this moment our dogs encountered a large male bear in the act of devouring a seal. The impulse was irresistible; I lost all control over both dogs and drivers. They seemed dead to everything but the passion of pursuit. Off they sped with incredible swiftness, the Esquimaux clinging to their sledges, and cheering their dogs with loud cries of "Nannook!" A mad, wild chase, wilder than German legend,—the dogs, wolves; the drivers, devils. After a furious run, the animal was brought to bay; the lance and the rifle did their work, and we halted for a general feed. The dogs gorged themselves, the drivers did as much, and we buried the remainder of the carcass in the snow. A second bear had been tracked by the party to a large iceberg north of Cape Russel; for we had now travelled to the neighbourhood of the Great Glacier. But the dogs were too much distended by their abundant diet to move: their drivers were scarcely better. Rest was indispensable.

We took a four hours' sleep on the open ice, the most uncomfortable that I remember. Our fatigue had made us dispense with the snow-house; and, though I was heavily clad in a full suit of furs, and squeezed myself in between Kalutunah and Shanghu, I could not bear the intense temperature. I rose in the morning stiff and sore. I mention it as a trait of nobleness on the part of Kalutunah, which I appreciated very sensibly at the time, that, seeing me suffer, he took his kapetah from his back and placed it around my feet.

The next day I tried again to make my friends steer to the northward. But the bears were most numerous upon the Greenland side; and they determined to push on toward the glacier. They were sure, they said, of finding the game among the broken icebergs at the base of it. All my remonstrances and urgent entreaties were unavailing to make them resume their promised route. They said that to cross so high up as we then were was impossible, and I felt the truth of this when I remembered the fate of poor Baker and Schubert at this very passage. Kalutunah added, significantly, that the bear-meat was absolutely necessary for the support of their families, and that Nalegak had no right to prevent him from providing for his household. It was a strong argument, and withal the argument of the strong.

I found now that my projected survey of the northern coast must be abandoned, at least for the time. My next wish was to get back to the brig, and to negotiate with Metek for a purchase or loan of his dogs as my last chance. But even this was not readily gratified. All of Saturday was spent in bear-hunting. The natives, as indomitable as their dogs, made the entire circuit of Dallas Bay, and finally halted again under one of the islands which group themselves between the headlands of Advance Bay and at the base of the glacier.

While the Esquimaux were hunting about the bergs, I sat and took a sketch of the glacier; seeing them come to a halt above the island, I gained the nearest sledge, and the whole party gathered together a few miles from the face of the glacier. Here Hans and myself crawled with

Tatterat and his dogs into an impromptu snow-hut, and, cheered by our aggregated warmth, slept comfortably. Our little dome, or rather burrow, for it was scooped out of a drift, fell down in the night; but we were so worn out that it did not wake us.

On rising from a sleep in the open air, at a temperature of 12° below zero, the hunt was resumed along the face of the glacier, with just enough of success to wear out the dogs and endanger my chances of return to the brig. In spite of the grandeur of the scenery and the noble displays of force exhibited by the falling bergs, my thoughts wandered back to the party I had left; and I was really glad when Kalutunah yielded to my renewed persuasion, and turned his team toward the ice-belt of the south-eastern shore.

The spot at which we landed I have called Cape James Kent. It was a lofty headland, and the land-ice which hugged its base was covered with rocks from the cliffs above. As I looked over this ice-belt, losing itself in the far distance, and covered with its millions of tons of rubbish, greenstones, limestones, chlorite slates, rounded and angular, massive and ground to powder, its importance as a geological agent in the transportation of drift struck me with great force. Its whole substance was studded with these varied contributions from the shore; and further to the south, upon the now frozen waters of Marshall Bay, I could recognise raft after raft from the last year's ice-belt, which had been caught by the winter, each one laden with its heavy freight of foreign material.

On the south-eastern corner of this bay, where some low islands at the mouth of the fiord formed a sort of protection against the north wind, was a group of Esquimaux remains,—huts, cairns, and graves. Though evidently long deserted, my drivers seemed to know all about them, for they suspended the hunt around the bergs to take a look at these evidences of a bygone generation of their fathers.

There were five huts, with two stone pedestals for the protection of meat, and one of those strange little kennels which serve as dormitories when the igloë is crowded. The graves were further up the fiord; from them I obtained a knife of bone, but no indications of iron.

These huts stood high up, upon a set of shingle-terraces, similar to those of Rensselaer Bay. The belt-ice at their foot was old and undisturbed, and must have been so for years; so, too, was the heavy ice of the bay. Yet around these old homesteads were bones of the seal and walrus, and the vertebræ of a whale similar to that of the igloë of Anoatok. There must have been both open water and a hunting-ground around them, and the huts had in former days been close upon this water-line. "Una suna nuna?" "What land is this, Kalutunah?" I did not understand his answer, which was long and emphatic; but I found from our interpreter that the place was still called "the inhabited spot;" and that a story was well preserved among them of a time when families were sustained beside its open water, and musk-ox inhabited the hills. We followed the belt-ice, crossing only at the headlands of the bays, and arrived at the brig on the afternoon of Wednesday.

The Esquimaux left the brig after a day's rest, fully laden with wood and other presents, and promising to engage Metek, if they could, to come up with his four dogs. They themselves engaged to lend me one dog from each of their teams. It pleased me to find that I had earned character with these people, at first so suspicious and distrustful. They left on board each man his dog, without a shade of doubt as to my good faith, only begging me to watch the poor animals' feet, as the famine had nearly exterminated their stock.

The month of May had come. Metek, less confiding because less trustworthy than Kalutunah, did not bring his dogs, and my own exhausted team was in almost daily requisition to bring in supplies of food from Etah. Everything admonished me that the time was at hand when we must leave the brig and trust our fortunes to the floes. Our preparations were well advanced, and the crew so far restored to health that all but three or four could take some part in completing them.

Still, I could not allow myself to pass away from our region of search without a last effort to visit the furthest shores of the channel. Our communications with the Esquimaux, and some successful hunts of our own, had given us a stock of provisions for at least a week in advance. I conferred with my officers, made a full distribution of the work to be performed in my absence, and set out once more, with Morton for my only companion. We took with us the light sledge, adding the two borrowed dogs to our team, but travelling ourselves on foot. Our course was to be by the middle ice, and our hope that we might find it free enough from hummocks to permit us to pass.

My journal, written after our return, gives nothing but a series of observations going to verify and complete my charts. We struggled manfully, through days and nights of adventurous exposure and recurring disaster, to force our way, and at last found our way back to the brig, Morton broken down anew, and my own energies just adequate to the duty of supervising our final departure. I had neither time nor strength to expend on my diary.

The operations of the search were closed.

The detailed preparations for our escape would have little interest for the general reader; but they were so arduous and so important that I cannot pass them by without a special notice. They had been begun from an early day of the fall, and had not been entirely intermitted during our severest winter-trials. All who could work, even at picking over eider-down, found every moment of leisure fully appropriated. But since our party had begun to develop the stimulus of more liberal diet, our labours were more systematic and diversified.

The manufacture of clothing had made considerable progress. Canvas mocassins had been made for every one of the party, and three dozen were added as a common stock to meet emergencies. Three pairs of boots were allowed each man. These were generally of carpeting, with soles of walrus and seal hide; and when the supply of these was exhausted, the leather from the chaffing-gear of the brig for a time supplied their place. A much better substitute was found afterward in the gutta-percha that had formed the speaking-tube. This was softened by warm water, cut into lengths, and so made available to its new uses. Blankets were served out as the material for body clothing. Every man was his own tailor.

For bedding, the woollen curtains that had formerly decorated our berths supplied us with a couple of large coverlets, which were abundantly quilted with eider-down. Two buffalo-robes of the same size, with the coverlets, were arranged so as to button on them, forming sleeping-sacks for the occasion, but easily detached for the purpose of drying or airing

Our provision-bags were of assorted sizes, to fit under the thwarts of the boats. They were of sail-cloth, made water-tight by tar and pitch, which we kept from penetrating the canvas by first coating it with flour-paste and plaster of Paris. The bread-bags were double, the inner saturated with paste and plaster by boiling in the mixture, and the space between the two filled with pitch. Every bag was, in sailor-phrase, roped and becketed; in ordinary parlance, well secured by cordage.

These different manufactures had all of them been going on through the winter, and more rapidly as the spring advanced. They had given employment to the thoughts of our sick men, and in this way had exerted a wholesome influence on their moral tone and assisted their convalescence. Other preparations had been begun more recently. The provisions for the descent were to be got ready and packed. The ship-bread was powdered by beating it with a capstan-bar, and pressed down into the bags which were to carry it. Pork-fat and tallow were melted down, and poured into other bags to freeze. A stock of concentrated bean-soup was cooked, and secured for carriage like the pork-fat; and the flour and remaining meat-biscuit were to be protected from moisture in double bags. These were the only provisions we were to carry with us. I knew I should be able to subsist the party for some time after their setting out by the food I could bring from the vessel by occasional trips with my dog-team. For the rest we relied upon our guns.

Besides all this, we had our camp equipage to get in order, and the vitally important organization of our system of boats and sledges.

Our boats were three in number, all of them well battered by exposure to ice and storm, almost as destructive of their seaworthiness as the hot sun of other regions. Two of them were cypress whaleboats, twenty-six feet long, with seven feet beam, and three feet deep. These were strengthened with oak bottom-pieces and a long stringpiece bolted to the keel. A wash board of light cedar, about six inches high, served to strengthen the gunwale and give increased depth. A neat housing of light canvas was stretched upon a ridge-line sustained fore and aft by stanchions, and hung down over the boats' sides, where it was fastened (stopped) to a jack-stay. My last year's experience on the attempt to reach Beechy Island determined me to carry but one mast to each boat. It was stepped into an oaken thwart, made especially strong, as it was expected to carry sail over ice as well as water; the mast could be readily unshipped, and carried, with the oars, boat-hooks, and ice-poles, alongside the boat. The third boat was my little *Red Eric*. We mounted her on the old sledge, the *Faith*, hardly relying on her for any purposes of navigation, but with the intention of cutting her up for firewood in case our guns should fail to give us a supply of blubber.

Indeed, in spite of all the ingenuity of our carpenter, Mr Ohlsen, well seconded by the persevering labours of M'Gary and Bonsall, not one of our boats was positively seaworthy. The *Hope* would not pass even charitable inspection, and we expected to burn her on reaching water. The planking of all of them was so dried it could hardly be made tight by calking.

The three boats were mounted on sledges rigged with rueraddies; the provisions stowed smugly under the thwarts; the chronometers carefully boxed and padded, placed in the stern sheets of the *Hope*, in charge of Mr Sontag. With them were such of the instruments as we could venture to transport.

Our powder and shot, upon which our lives depended, were carefully distributed in bags and tin canisters. The percussion-caps I took into my own possession, as more precious than gold. Mr Bonsall had a general charge of the arms and ammunition. Places were arranged for the guns, and hunters appointed for each boat. Mr Petersen took charge of the most important part of our field-equipage, our cooking gear. Petersen was our best tinker. All the old stove-pipe, now none the better for two winters of Arctic fires, was called into requisition. Each boat was provided with two large iron cylinders, fourteen inches in diameter and eighteen high. Each of them held an iron saucer or lamp, in which we could place our melted pork-fat or blubber, and, with the aid of spun-yarn for a wick, make a roaring fire. I need not say that the fat and oil always froze when not ignited.

Into these cylinders, which were used merely to defend our lamp from the wind, and our pots from contact with the cold air, we placed a couple of large tin vessels, suitable either for melting snow or making tea or soup. They were made out of cake-canisters cut down. How many kindly festival associations hung by these now abused soup-cans! One of them had, before the fire rubbed off its bright gilding, the wedding inscription of a large fruit-cake.

We carried spare tins in case the others should burn out; it was well we did so. So completely had we exhausted our household furniture, that we had neither cups nor plates, except crockery. This, of course, would not stand the travel, and our spare tin had to be saved for protecting the boats from ice. At this juncture we cut plates out of every imaginable and rejected piece of tinware. Borden's meat-biscuit canisters furnished us with a splendid dinner-service; and some rightly-feared tin jars, with ominous labels of Corrosive Sublimate and Arsenic, which once belonged to our department of natural history, were emptied, scoured, and cut down into tea-cups.

Recognising the importance of acting directly upon the men's minds, my first step now was to issue a general order appointing a certain day, the 17th of May, for setting out. Every man had twenty-four hours given him to select and get ready his eight pounds of personal effects. After that, his time was to cease to be his own for any purpose. The long-indulged waywardness of our convalescents made them take this hardly. Some who were at work on articles of apparel that were really important to them threw them down unfinished, in a sick man's pet. I had these in some cases picked up quietly and finished by others. But I showed myself inexorable. It was necessary to brace up and concentrate every man's thoughts and energies upon the one great common object, our departure from the vessel on the 17th, not to return.

I tried my best also to fix and diffuse impressions that we were going home. But in this I was not always successful. I was displeased, indeed, with the moody indifference with which many went about the tasks to which I put them. The completeness of my preparations I know had its influence; but there were many doubters. Some were convinced that my only object was to move further south, retaining the brig, however, as a home to retreat to. Others whispered that I wanted to transport the sick to the hunting-grounds and other resources of the lower settlements. A few of a more cheerful spirit thought I had resolved to make for some point of look-out, in the hope of a rescue by whalers or English expedition parties which were supposed still to be within the Arctic circle. The number is unfortunately small of those human beings whom calamity elevates.

There was no sign or affectation of spirit or enthusiasm upon the memorable day when we first adjusted the boats to their cradles on the sledges and moved them off to the ice-foot. But the ice immediately around the vessel was smooth; and, as the boats had not received their lading, the first labour was an easy one. As the runners moved, the gloom of several countenances were perceptibly lightened. The croakers had protested that we could not stir an inch. These cheering remarks always reach a commander's ears, and I took good care of course to make the outset contradict them. By the time we reached the end of our little level, the tone had improved wonderfully, and we were prepared for the effort of crossing the successive lines of the belt-ice and forcing a way through the smashed material which interposed between us and the ice-foot.

This was a work of great difficulty, and sorrowfully exhausting to the poor fellows not yet accustomed to heave together. But in the end I had the satisfaction, before twenty-four hours were over, of seeing our little arks of safety hauled upon the higher plane of the ice-foot, in full trim for ornamental exhibition from the brig; their neat canvas-housing rigged, tent-fashion, over the entire length of each; a jaunty little flag, made out of one of the commander's obsolete linen shirts, decorated in stripes from a disused article of stationery, the red-ink bottle, and with a very little of the blue-bag in the star-spangled corner. All hands after this returned on board; I had ready for them the best supper our supplies afforded, and they turned in with minds prepared for their departure next day.

They were nearly all of them invalids, unused to open air and exercise. It was necessary to train them very gradually. We made but two miles the first day, and with a single boat; and indeed for some time after this I took care that they should not be disheartened by overwork. They came back early to a hearty supper and warm beds, and I had the satisfaction of marching them back each recurring morning refreshed and cheerful. The weather, happily, was superb.

CHAPTER XVII.

FAREWELL TO THE "ADVANCE."

Our last farewell to the brig was made with more solemnity. The entire ship's company was collected in our dismantled winter-chamber to take part in the ceremonial. It was Sunday. Our moss walls had been torn down, and the wood that supported them burned. Our beds were off at the boats. The galley was unfurnished and cold. Everything about the little den of refuge was desolate.

We read prayers and a chapter of the Bible; and then, all standing silently round, I took Sir John Franklin's portrait from its frame and cased it in an India-rubber scroll. I next read the reports of inspection and survey which had been made by the several commissions organized for the purpose, all of them testifying to the necessities under which I was about to act. I then addressed the party: I did not affect to disguise the difficulties that were before us; but I assured them that they could all be overcome by energy and subordination to command; and that the thirteen hundred miles of ice and water that lay between us and North Greenland could be traversed with safety for most of us, and hope for all. I added, that as men and messmates, it was the duty of us all, enjoined by gallantry as well as religion, to postpone every consideration of self to the protection of the wounded and sick; and that this must be regarded by every man, and under all circumstances, as a paramount order. In conclusion, I told them to think over the trials we had all of us gone through, and to remember each man for himself how often an unseen Power had rescued him in peril; and I admonished them still to place reliance on Him who could not change.

I was met with a right spirit. After a short conference, an engagement was drawn up by one of the officers, and brought to me with the signatures of all the company, without an exception. It read as follows:—

"SECOND GRINNELL EXPEDITION,
"BRIG 'ADVANCE,' *May* 20, 1855.

"The undersigned, being convinced of the impossibility of the liberation of the brig, and equally convinced of the impossibility of remaining in the ice a third winter, do fervently concur with the commander in his attempt to reach the south by means of boats.

"Knowing the trials and hardships which are before us, and feeling the necessity of union, harmony, and discipline, we have determined to abide faithfully by the expedition and our sick comrades, and to do all that we can, as true men, to advance the objects in view.

"HENRY BROOKS,   J. WALL WILSON,
JAMES M'GARY,   AMOS BONSALL,
GEORGE RILEY,   I. I. HAYES,
WILLIAM MORTON,   AUGUST SONTAG,
C. OHLSEN,   &c., &c."

I had prepared a brief memorial of the considerations which justified our abandonment of the vessel, and had read it as part of my address. I now fixed it to a stanchion near the gangway, where it must attract the notice of any who might seek us hereafter, and stand with them as my vindication for the step, in case we should be overtaken by disaster. It closed with these words:—

"I regard the abandonment of the brig as inevitable. We have by actual inspection but thirty-six days' provisions, and a careful survey shows that we cannot cut more firewood without rendering our craft unseaworthy. A third winter would force us, as the only means of escaping starvation, to resort to Esquimaux habits and give up all hope of remaining by the vessel and her resources. It would therefore in no manner advance the search after Sir John Franklin.

"Under any circumstances, to remain longer would be destructive to those of our little party who have already suffered from the extreme severity of the climate and its tendencies to disease. Scurvy has enfeebled more or less every man in the expedition; and an anomalous spasmodic disorder, allied to tetanus, has cost us the life of two of our most prized comrades.

"I hope, speaking on the part of my companions and myself, that we have done all that we ought to do to prove our tenacity of purpose and devotion to the cause which we have undertaken. This attempt to escape by crossing the southern ice on sledges is regarded by me as an imperative duty,—the only means of saving ourselves and preserving the laboriously-earned results of the expedition.

"E. K. KANE,
"Commander, Grinnell Expedition.

"'ADVANCE,' RENSSELAER BAY, *May* 20, 1855."

We then went upon deck: the flags were hoisted and hauled down again, and our party walked once or twice around the brig, looking at her timbers and exchanging comments upon the scars which reminded them of every stage of her dismantling. Our figure-head—the fair Augusta, the little blue girl with pink cheeks, who had lost her breast by an iceberg and her nose by a nip off Bedevilled Reach—was taken from our bows and placed aboard the "Hope." "She is at any rate wood," said the men, when I hesitated about giving them the additional burden; "and if we cannot carry her far we can burn her."

No one thought of the mockery of cheers: we had no festival-liquor to mislead our perception of the real state of things. When all hands were quite ready, we scrambled off over the ice together, much like a gang of stevedores going to work over a quayful of broken cargo.

Excluding four sick men, who were unable to move, and myself, who had to drive the dog-team and serve as common carrier and courier, we numbered but twelve men,—which would have given six to a sledge, or too few to move it. It was therefore necessary to concentrate our entire force upon one sledge at a time. On the other hand, however, it was important to the efficiency of our organization that matters of cooking, sleeping baggage, and rations, should be regulated by separate messes.

The routine I established was the most precise:—Daily prayers both morning and evening, all hands gathering round in a circle and standing uncovered during the short exercise; regulated hours; fixed duties and positions at the track-lines and on the halt; the cooking to be taken by turns, the captains of the boats alone being excused. The charge of the log was confided to Dr Hayes, and the running survey to Mr Sontag. Though little could be expected from either of these gentlemen at this time, I deemed it best to keep up the appearance of ordinary voyaging; and after we left the first ices of Smith's Straits I was indebted to them for valuable results. The thermometer was observed every three hours.

To my faithful friend and first officer, boatswain Brooks, I assigned the command of the boats and sledges. I knew how well he was fitted for it; and when forced, as I was afterward during the descent, to be in constant motion between the sick-station, the Esquimaux settlements, and the deserted brig, I felt safe in the assurance of his tried fidelity and indomitable resolution. The party under him was marshalled at the rue-raddies as a single gang; but the messes were arranged with reference to the two whale-boats, and when we came afterward to the open water the crews distributed in the same way:—

To the *Faith*.	To the *Hope*.
JAMES M'GARY,	WILLIAM MORTON,
CHRISTIAN OHLSEN,	AUGUST SONTAG,
AMOS BONSALL,	GEORGE RILEY,
CARL J. PETERSEN,	JOHN BLAKE,
THOMAS HICKEY.	WILLIAM GODFREY.

With this organization we set out on our march.

Up to the evening of the 23d, the progress was little more than a mile a day for one sledge; on the 24th, both sledges reached First Ravine, a distance of seven miles, when we found that the dog-sledge had brought on to this station the buffalo bags and other sleeping appliances which we had prepared during the winter. The condition of the party was such that it was essential they should sleep in comfort; and it was a rule, therefore, during the whole journey, never departed from unless in extreme emergency, never to begin a new day's labour till the party was refreshed from the exertions of the day before. Our halts were regulated by the condition of the men rather than by arbitrary hours, and sleep was meted out in proportion to the trials of the march. We slept by day when the sun was warmest, and travelled when we could avoid his greatest glare.

Mr Morton, Ohlsen, and Petersen, during this time performed a double duty. They took their turn at the sledges with the rest, but they were also engaged in preparing the *Red Eric* as a comrade boat. She was mounted on our good old sledge, the *Faith*—a sledge that, like her namesake, our most reliable whaleboat, had been our very present help in many times of trouble. I believe every man felt, when he saw her brought out, that stout work was to be done, and under auspices of good.

In the meantime I had carried Mr Goodfellow, with my dog-sledge, to a sick-station, which I had arranged at Anoatok; and had managed to convey the rest one by one to the same spot. Mr Wilson, whose stump was still unhealed, and who suffered besides from scurvy; George Whipple, whose tendons were so contracted that he could not extend his legs, and poor Stephenson, just able to keep the lamps burning and warm up food for the rest, were the other invalids, all incapable of moving without assistance.

It is just that I should speak of the manly fortitude with which they bore up during this painful imprisonment. Dr Hayes, though still disabled from his frozen foot, adhered manfully to the sledges.

As I review my notes of the first few days of our ice-journey, I find them full of incidents, interesting and even momentous when they occurred, but which cannot claim a place in this narrative. The sledges were advancing slowly, the men often discouraged, and now and then one giving way under the unaccustomed labour.

The *Red Boat* was completed for service in a few days, and joined the sledge-party on the floes,—an additional burden, but a necessary one, for our weary rue-raddies; and I set out for the sick-station with Mr Goodfellow, our last remaining invalid. As my team reached the entrance of Force Bay, I saw that poor Nessark, the Esquimaux, who had carried Mr Wilson and some stores to Anoatok, finding his sledge-load too heavy, had thrown out a portion of it upon the ice. He had naturally enough selected the bread for his jettison, an article of diet unknown among the Esquimaux, but precisely that of which our sick were most in need. I lost some time in collecting such parts of his rejected cargo as I could find, and, when I reached the huts after a twelve hours' drive, the condition of our sick men made it imperative that I should return at once to the brig. The strength of the dogs began to fail while crossing the reach of Force Bay, and I was forced to camp out with them on the ice-belt, but early in the morning I came upon the fires of the sledge-party.

The men were at prayers when I first saw them ; but, as they passed to the drag-ropes, I was pained to see how wearily they moved. Poor Brooks' legs were so swollen that he could not brace them in his blanket coverings, and

Dr Hayes could hardly keep his place. The men generally showed symptoms of increasing scurvy. It was plain that they could not hold their own without an increased allowance, if not of meat, at least of fresh bread and hot tea.

Taking with me Morton, my faithful adjutant always, I hurried on to the brig.

We lighted fires in the galley, melted pork, baked a large batch of bread, gathered together a quantity of beans and dried apples, somewhat damaged, but still eatable, and by the time our dogs had fed and rested, we were ready for the return. Distributing our supplies as we passed the squads on the floe, I hastened to Anoatok. I had taken Godfrey with us from his party, and, as it was painfully evident that the men could not continue to work without more generous food, I sent him on to Etah with the dogs, in the hope of procuring a stock of walrus-meat.

The little company at the hut welcomed my return. They had exhausted their provisions; their lamp had gone out; the snow-drift had forced its way in at the door, so that they could not close it; it was blowing a north-easter; and the thermometer, which hung against the blanketed walls, stood only sixteen degree above zero. The poor fellows had all the will to protect themselves, but they were lame, and weak, and hungry, and disheartened. We built a fire for them of tarred rope, dried their bedding, cooked them a porridge of meat-biscuit and pea-soup, fastened up their desolate door-way, hung a dripping-slab of pork-fat over their lamp-wick, and, first joining in a prayer of thankfulness, and then a round of merry gossip, all hands forgot sickness, and privation, and distance in the contentment of our sleeping-bags. I cannot tell how long we slept, for all our watches ran down before we awoke.

The gale had risen, and it was snowing hard when I replenished the fires of our heartstone. But we went on burning rope and fat, in a regular tea-drinking frolic, till not an icicle or even a frost-mark was to be seen on the roof. After a time Godfrey rejoined us; Metek came with him; and between their two sledges they brought an ample supply of meat. With part of this I hastened to the sledge-party. They were now off Ten-mile Ravine, struggling through the accumulated snows, and much exhausted, though not out of heart. In spite of their swollen feet, they had worked fourteen hours a day, passing in that time over some twelve miles of surface, and advancing a mile and a half on their way.

Once more leaving the party on the floe, Morton and myself, with Metek and his sledge in company, revisited the brig, and set ourselves to work baking bread. The brig was dreary enough, and Metek was glad to bid it good-bye, with one hundred and fifty pounds on his dog-sledge, consigned to Mr Brooks. But he carried besides a letter, safely trusted to his inspection, which directed that he should be sent back forthwith for another load. It was something like a breach of faith, perhaps; but his services were indispensable, and his dogs still more so. He returned, of course, for there was no escaping us; his village lay in the opposite direction, and he could not deviate from the track after once setting out. In the meantime we had cooked about a hundred pounds of flour pudding, and tried out a couple of bagfuls of pork-fat,— a good day's work,—and we were quite ready, before the subdued brightness of midnight came, to turn in to our beds. Our beds!—there was not an article of covering left on board. We ripped open the old mattresses, and, all three crawling down among the curled hair, Morton, Metek, and the Nalegak, slept as sound as vagrants on a hay-stack.

On Monday, the 28th, we all set out for the boats and Anoatok. Both Metek and myself had all our sledges heavily laden. We carried the last of our provision-bags, completing now our full complement of fifteen hundred pounds, the limit of capacity of our otherwise crowded boats.

It caused me a bitter pang to abandon our collection of objects of natural history, the cherished fruit of so much exposure and toil; and it was hardly easier to leave some other things behind,—several of my well-tested instruments, for instance, and those silent friends, my books. They had all been packed up, hoping for a chance of saving them; and, to the credit of my comrades, let me say gratefully that they offered to exclude both clothes and food in favour of a full freight of these treasures.

But the thing was not to be thought of. I gave a last look at the desolate galley-stove, the representative of our long winter's fireside, at the still bright coppers now full of frozen water, the theodolite, the chart-box, and poor Wilson's guitar,—once more at the remnant of the old moss-walls, the useless daguerreotypes, and the skeletons of dog, and deer, and bear, and musk-ox,—stoppered in the rigging;—and, that done, whipped up my dogs so much after the manner of a sentimentalising Christian, that our pagan Metek raised a prayer in their behalf.

CHAPTER XVII.

THE MARCH AND ITS INCIDENTS.

I found that Mr Brooks had succeeded in getting his boat and sledges as far as the floe off Bedevilled Reach. I stopped only long enough to point out to him an outside track, where I had found the ice quite smooth and free from snow, and pressed my dogs for the hut. I noticed, to my great joy, too, that the health of his party seemed to be improving under our raw-meat specific, and could not find fault with the extravagant use they were making of it.

The invalids at the sick-station were not as well as I could have wished; but I had only time to renew their stock of provision and give them a few cheering words. Our walrus-meat was nearly exhausted.

I had fixed upon two new stations further to the south, as the depôts to which our stores were now to be transported. One was upon the old and heavy floes off Navialik, "the big gull's place,"—a headland opposite Cape Hatherton,—the other on the level ice-plain near Littleton Island. Having now gathered our stores at Anoatok, I began with a thankful heart to move them onward. I sent on Metek to the further station with two bags of bread-dust, each weighing ninety pounds, and, having myself secured some three hundred pounds at Navialik, drove on for Etah Bay.

My long succession of journeys on this route had made me thoroughly weary of the endless waste of ice to seaward, and I foolishly sought upon this trip to vary the travel by following the ice-belt. But, upon reaching Refuge Harbour, I found the snow so heavy and the fragments from the cliffs so numerous and threatening, that I was obliged to give it up. A large chasm stopped my advance and drove me out again upon the floes.

Getting beyond a table-land known as Kasarsoak, or "the big promontory," I emerged from the broken ice upon a wide plain. Here I first saw with alarm that the ice had changed its character: the snow which covered it had become lead-coloured and sodden by the water from beneath, and ice-fields after ice-fields stretching before me were all covered with stained patches. As I rode along these lonely marshes, for such they were, the increased labour of the dogs admonished me that the floe was no longer to be trusted. It chilled my heart to remember the position of our boats and stores. Nearly nine hundred pounds of food, exclusive of the load now upon my sledge, were still awaiting transportation at Anoatok.

Two hundred more, including our shot and bullet-bags, were at the Cape Hatherton station; and Metek's load was probably by this time lying on the ice opposite M'Gary Island. Like Robinson Crusoe with his powder, the reflection came over me:—"Good God! what will become of us if all this is destroyed?"

Only by men experienced in the rapid changes of Arctic ice can the full force of this reflection be appreciated. A single gale might convert the precarious platform, over which we were travelling, into a tumultuous ice-pack. Had the boats their stores on board even, and could they break through without foundering, there was not the remotest prospect of their being liberated in open water; and I knew well what obstacles a wet, sludy surface would present to our over-tasked and almost worn-out party.

I determined, therefore, as soon as I could secure the meat, which was my immediate errand, to make a requisition upon the Esquimaux for two of the four dogs which were still at Etah, and by their aid to place the provisions in safety. The north cape of Littleton Island, afterward called Point Security, was selected for the purpose, and I left orders with the invalids at the sick station to be in readiness for instant removal. I pursued my journey alone.

It was quite late in the evening when I drew near Etah. I mean that it was verging on to our midnight, the sun being low in the heavens, and the air breathing that solemn stillness which belongs to the sleeping-time of birds and plants. I had not quite reached the little settlement when loud sounds of laughter came to my ear; and, turning the cape, I burst suddenly upon an encampment of the inhabitants.

Some thirty men, women, and children, were gathered together upon a little face of offal-stained rock. Except a bank of moss, which broke the wind-draught from the fiord, they were entirely without protection from the weather, though the temperature was 5° below zero. The huts were completely deserted, the snow-tossut had fallen in, and the window was as free and open as summer to the purifying air. Every living thing about the settlement was out upon the bare rocks.

The fires were of peat-moss, greased with the fat of the bird-skins. They were used only for cooking, however, the people depending for comfort on the warmth of close contact. Old Kresut, the blind patriarch of the settlement, was the favoured centre, and around him, as a focus, was a coil of men, women, and children, as perplexing to unravel as a skein of eels. The children alone were toddling about and bringing in stores of moss, their faces smeared with blood, and tit-bits of raw liver between their teeth.

The scene was redolent of plenty and indolence,—the *dolce far niente* of the short-lived Esquimaux summer. Provision for the dark winter was furthest from their thoughts; for, although the rocks were patched with sun-dried birds, a single hunting-party from Peteravik could have eaten up their entire supplies in a night.

The dogs seemed as happy as their masters: they were tethered by seal-skin thongs to prevent robbery, but evidently fed to the full extent of their capacity.

Aningnah, wife of Marsumah, was one of the presiding deities of the soup-pot, or rather first witch of the caldron. She was a tall, well-made woman, and, next to Mrs Metek, had a larger influence than any female in the settlement.

During one of my visits to the settlement, I had relieved her from much suffering by opening a furuncle, and the kind creature never lost an opportunity of showing how she remembered it. Poor old Kresut was summarily banished from his central seat of honour, and the nalegak installed in his place. She stripped herself of her bird-skin kapetah to make me a coverlet, and gave me her two-year-old baby for a pillow. There was a little commotion in the tangled mass of humanity as I crawled over them to accept these proffered hospitalities; but it was all of a welcoming sort. I had learned by this time to take kindly and condescendingly the privileges of my rank; and, with my inner man well refreshed with auk-livers, I was soon asleep.

In the morning I left my own tired dogs in charge of Marsumah, quite confident that his wife would feed them faithfully, and took from them their only team in unequal exchange. Such had become our relations with these poor friends of ours, that such an act of authority would have gone unquestioned if it had cost them a much graver sacrifice. They saw the condition of my own travel-broken animals, and were well aware of the sufferings of our party, so long their neighbours and allies. Old Nessark filled my sledge with walrus-meat; and two of the young men joined me on foot, to assist me through the broken ice between Littleton Island and the mainland.

The sledge-party under Mr Brooks had advanced to within three miles of the hut when I reached them on my return. They had found the ice more practicable, and their health was improving. But their desire for food had increased proportionally; and, as it was a well-understood rule of our commissariat not to touch the reserved provision of the boats, it became necessary to draw additional supplies from the brig. The seven hundred pounds of bread-dust, our entire stock, could not be reduced with safety.

But the dogs were wanted to advance the contents of our Anoatok storehouse to the stations further south, and I resolved to take Tom Hickey with me and walk back for another baking exploit. It was more of an effort than I counted on: we were sixteen hours on the ice, and we had forgotten our gutta-percha eyantick, or slit-goggles. The glare of the sun as we entered the curve of our ice-cumbered harbour almost blinded us.

Tom had been a baker at home; but he assures me, with all the authority of an ancient member of the guild, that our achievement the day we came on board might be worthy of praise in the "old country;" Tom knows no praise more expanded. We kneaded the dough in a large pickled-cabbage cask, burnt sundry volumes of the "Penny Cyclopædia of Useful Knowledge," and converted, between duff and loaf, almost a whole barrel of flour into a strong likeness to the staff of life. It was the last of our stock; and "all the better too," said my improvident comrade, who retained some of the genius of blundering as well as the gallantry of his countrymen,—"all the better, sir, since we'll have no more bread to bake."

Godfrey came on with the dogs three days after, to carry back the fruits of our labour; but an abrupt change of the weather gave us a howling gale outside, and we were all of us storm-stayed. It was Sunday, and probably the last time that two or three would be gathered together in our dreary cabin. So I took a Bible from one of the bunks, and we went through the old-times service. It was my closing act of official duty among my shipmates on board the poor little craft. I visited her afterward, but none of them were with me.

I was glad, when I reached the sick-station, to find things so much better. Everybody was stronger, and, as a consequence, more cheerful. They had learned housekeeping, with its courtesies as well as comforts. Their kotluk would have done credit to Aningnah herself: they had a dish of tea for us, and a lump of walrus; and they bestirred themselves, real housewife-fashion, to give us the warm place and make us comfortable. I was right sorry to leave them, for the snow outside was drifting with the gale; but after a little while the dogs struck the track of the sledges, and following it with unerring instinct, did not slacken their pace till they had brought us to our companions on the floe.

They had wisely halted on account of the storm; and, with their three little boats drawn up side by side for mutual protection, had been lying to for the past two days, tightly housed, and moored fast by whale-lines to the ice. But the drifts had almost buried the *Hope*, which was the windward boat; and when I saw the burly form of Brooks emerging from the snow-covered roof, I could have fancied it a walrus rising through the ice.

They had found it hard travel, but were doing well. Brooks's provision-report was the old story,—out of meat and nearly out of bread—no pleasant news for a tired-out man, who saw in this the necessity of another trip to Etah. I was only too glad, however, to see that their appetites held, for with the animal man, as with all others, while he feeds he lives.

Six Esquimaux, three of them women—that ugly beauty, Nessark's wife, at the head of them—had come off to the boats for shelter from the gale. They seemed so entirely deferential, and to recognise with such simple trust our mutual relations of alliance, that I resolved to drive down to Etah with Petersen as interpreter, and formally claim assistance, according to their own laws, on the ground of our established brotherhood. I had thought of this before; but both Marsumah and Metek had been so engrossed with their bird-catching that I was loath to take them from their families.

After further consideration, I determined to send Morton; so Petersen and myself gave up the sledge to him, and, along with Marsumah and Nessark, he set out at once to negotiate at Etah, while I took my place with the sledge-parties.

The 6th saw the same disheartening work. The ice was almost impassable. Both sick and well worked at the drag-ropes alike, and hardly a man but was constantly wet to the skin. Fearing for the invalids at the sick-station in case we should be cut off from them, I sent for Mr Goodfellow at once, and gave orders for the rest to be in readiness for removal at a moment's notice.

The next day Morton returned from Etah. The natives had responded to the brotherly appeal of the nalegak; and they came down from the settlement, bringing a full supply of meat and blubber, and every sound dog that belonged to them. I had now once more a serviceable team. The comfort and security of such a possession to men in our critical position can hardly be realised. It was more than an addition of ten strong men to our party. I set off at once with Metek to glean from the brig her last remnant of slush (tallow), and to bring down the sick men from Anoatok.

Our visit to the brig was soon over: we had very few stores to remove. I trod her solitary deck for the last time, and returned with Metek to his sledge.

I had left the party on the floes with many apprehensions for their safety, and the result proved they were not without cause. While crossing a "tide-hole," one of the runners of the *Hope's* sledge broke through, and, but for the strength and presence of mind of Ohlsen, the boat would have gone under. He saw the ice give way, and, by a violent exercise of strength, passed a capstan-bar under the sledge, and thus bore the load till it was hauled on to safer ice. He was a very powerful man, and might have done this without injuring himself; but it would seem his footing gave way under him, forcing him to make a still more desperate effort to extricate himself. It cost him his life—he died three days afterwards.

I was bringing down George Stephenson from the sick-station, and my sledge being heavily laden, I had just crossed, with some anxiety, near the spot at which the accident occurred. A little way beyond we met Mr Ohlsen, seated upon a lump of ice, and very pale. He pointed to the camp about three miles further on, and told us, in a faint voice, that he had not detained the party; he "had a little cramp in the small of the back," but would soon be better.

I put him at once in Stephenson's place, and drove him on to the *Faith*. Here he was placed in the stern-sheets of the boat, and well muffled up in our best buffalo-robes. During all that night he was assiduously attended by Dr Hayes; but he sank rapidly. His symptoms had from the first a certain obscure but fatal resemblance to our winter's tetanus, which filled us with forebodings.

On Saturday, June 6, after stowing away our disabled comrade in the *Faith*, we again set all hands at the drag-ropes. The ice ahead of us bore the same character as the day before—no better; we were all perceptibly weaker, and much disheartened.

We had been tugging in harness about two hours, when a breeze set in from the northward, the first that we had felt since crossing Bedevilled Reach. We got out our long steering-oar as a boom, and made sail upon the boats. The wind freshened almost to a gale; and, heading toward the depôt on Littleton Island, we ran gallantly before it.

It was a new sensation to our foot-sore men, this sailing over solid ice. Levels which, under the slow labour of the drag-ropes, would have delayed us for hours, were glided over without a halt. We thought it dangerous work at first, but the speed of the sledges made rotten ice nearly as available as sound. The men could see plainly that they were approaching new landmarks, and leaving old ones behind. Their spirits rose; the sick mounted the thwarts, the well clung to the gunwale; and, for the first time for nearly a year, broke out the sailor's chorus, " Storm along, my hearty boys !"

We must have made a greater distance in this single day than in the five that preceded it. We encamped at 5 P.M. near a small berg, which gave us plenty of fresh water, after a progress of at least eight miles.

As we were halting, I saw two Esquimaux on the ice toward Life-Boat Cove; and the well-known "Huk! huuk!" a sort of masonic signal among them, soon brought them to us. They turned out to be Sip-su and old Nessark. They were the bearers of good news: my dogs were refreshed and nearly able to travel again; and, as they volunteered to do me service, I harnessed up our united teams, and despatched Nessark to the hut to bring down Mr Wilson and George Whipple.

We expected now to have our whole party together again; and the day would have been an active cheering one throughout, but for the condition of poor Ohlsen, who was growing rapidly worse.

From this time we went on for some days, aided by our sails, meeting with accidents occasionally—the giving way of a spar or the falling of some of the party through the spongy ice—and occasionally, when the floe was altogether too infirm, labouring our way with great difficulty upon the ice-belt.

One only was absent of all the party that remained on our rolls. Hans, the kind son and ardent young lover of Fiskernaes, my well-trusted friend, had been missing for nearly two months. I am loath to tell the story as I believe it, for it may not be the true one after all, and I would not intimate an unwarranted doubt of the constancy of boyish love. But I must explain, as far as I can at least, why he was not with us when we first looked at the open water. Just before my departure for my April hunt, Hans came to me with a long face, asking permission to visit Peteravik: "he had no boots, and wanted to lay in a stock of walrus-hide for soles; he did not need the dogs; he would rather walk." It was a long march, but he was well practised in it, and I consented of course. Both

Petersen and myself gave him commissions to execute, and he left us, intending to stop by the way at Etah.

In our labours of the next month we missed Hans much. He had not yet returned, and the stories of him that came to us from Etah were the theme of much conversation and surmise among us. He had certainly called there as he promised, and given to Nessark's wife an order for a pair of boots, and he had then wended his way across the big headland to Peteravik, where Shang-hu and his pretty daughter had their home. This intimation was given with many an explanatory grin; for Hans was a favourite with all, the fair especially, and, as a *match*, one of the greatest men in the country. It required all my recollections of his "old love" to make me suspend my judgment; for the boots came, as if to confirm the scandal. I never failed in my efforts afterward to find his whereabouts, and went out of our way to interrogate this and that settlement; for, independent of everything like duty, I was very fond of him. But the story was everywhere the same. Hans the faithful—yet, I fear, the faithless—was last seen upon a native sledge, driving south from Peteravik, with a maiden at his side, and professedly bound to a new principality at Uwarrow Suk-suk, high up Murchison's Sound. Alas for Hans, the married man!

Though the condition of the ice assured us that we were drawing near the end of our sledge-journeys, it by no means diminished their difficulty or hazards. The part of the field near the open water is always abraded by the currents, while it remains apparently firm on the surface. In some places it was so transparent that we could even see the gurgling eddies below it; while in others it was worn into open holes that were already the resort of wild fowl. But in general it looked hard and plausible, though no more than a foot or even six inches in thickness.

This continued to be its character as long as we pursued the Littleton Island channel, and we were compelled, the whole way through, to sound ahead with the boat-hook or narwhal-horn. We learned this precaution from the Esquimaux, who always move in advance of their sledges when the ice is treacherous, and test its strength before bringing on their teams. Our first warning impressed us with the policy of observing it. We were making wide circuits with the whale-boats to avoid the tide-holes, when signals of distress from men scrambling on the ice announced to us that the *Red Eric* had disappeared. This unfortunate little craft contained all the dearly-earned documents of the expedition. There was not a man who did not feel that the reputation of the party rested in a great degree upon their preservation. It had cost us many a pang to give up our collections of natural history, to which every one had contributed his quota of labour and interest; but the destruction of the vouchers of the cruise—the log-books, the meteorological registers, the surveys, and the journals—seemed to strike them all as an irreparable disaster.

When I reached the boat everything was in confusion. Blake, with a line passed round his waist, was standing up to his knees in sludge, groping for the document-box; and Mr Bonsall, dripping wet, was endeavouring to haul the provision-bags to a place of safety. Happily the boat was our lightest one, and everything was saved. She was gradually lightened until she could bear a man, and her cargo was then passed out by a line and hauled upon the ice. In spite of the wet and the cold, and our thoughts of poor Ohlsen, we greeted its safety with three cheers.

It was by great good fortune that no lives were lost. Stephenson was caught as he sank by one of the sledge-runners, and Morton, while in the very act of drifting under the ice, was seized by the hair of the head by Mr Bonsall and saved.

We were now close upon Life-boat Cove, where nearly two years before we had made provision for just such a contingency as that which was now before us. Buried under the frozen soil, our stores had escaped even the keen scrutiny of our savage allies, and we now turned to them as essential to our relief. Mr M'Gary was sent to the *cache*, with orders to bring everything except the salt beef. This had been so long a poison to us that, tainted as we were by scurvy, I was afraid to bring it among those who might be tempted to indulge in it.

On the 12th the boats and sledges came to a halt in the narrow passage between the islands opposite Cape Misery, the scene of our late snow storm. All our cargo had been gathered together at this spot, and the rocks were covered with our stores. Out of the fourteen hundred pounds not an ounce had been sacrificed. Everything was cased in its waterproof covering, and as dry and perfect as when it had left the brig.

I was with the advance boat, trying to force a way through the channel, when the report came to me from Dr Hayes that Ohlsen was no more. He had shown, a short half hour before, some signs of revival, and Petersen had gone out to kill a few birds, in the hope of possibly sustaining him by a concentrated soup. But it was in vain: the poor fellow flushed up only to die a few minutes after.

We had no time to mourn the loss of our comrade, a tried and courageous man, who met his death in the gallant discharge of duty. It cast a gloom over the whole party;

but the exigencies of the moment were upon us, and we knew not whose turn would come next, or how soon we might all of us follow him together.

The body of Mr Ohlsen was sewed up, while they were gone, in his own blankets, and carried in procession to the head of a little gorge on the east face of Pekiutlik, where by hard labour we consigned his remains to a sort of trench, and covered them with rocks to protect them from the fox and bear. Without the knowledge of my comrades, I encroached on our little store of sheet-lead, which we were husbanding to mend our leaky boats with, and, cutting on a small tablet his name and age—

CHRISTIAN OHLSEN,

AGED 36 YEARS,

laid it on his manly breast. The cape that looks down on him bears his name.

We gave two quiet hours to the memory of our dead brother, and then resumed our toilsome march. We kept up nearly the same routine as before; but, as we neared the settlements, the Esquimaux came in flocks to our assistance. They volunteered to aid us at the drag-ropes. They carried our sick upon hand-sledges. They relieved us of all care for our supplies of daily food. The quantity of little auks that they brought us was enormous. They fed us and our dogs at the rate of eight thousand birds a week, all of them caught in their little hand-nets. All anxiety left us for the time. The men broke out in their old forecastle songs; the sledges began to move merrily ahead, and laugh and jest drove out the old moody silence.

My little note-book closes for the week with this gratefully-expounded record:—

"*June* 16.—Our boats are at the open water. We see its deep indigo horizon, and hear its roar against the icy beach. Its scent is in our nostrils and our hearts.

"Our camp is but three-quarters of a mile from the sea; it is at the northern curve of the North Baffin polynia. We must reach it at the southern sweep of Etah Bay, about three miles from Cape Alexander. A dark headland defines the spot. It is more marked than the southern entrance of Smith's Straits. How magnificently the surf beats against its sides! There are ridges of squeezed ice between us and it, and a broad zone of floating sludge is swelling and rolling sluggishly along its margin—formidable barriers to boats and sledges. But we have mastered worse obstacles, and by God's help we will master these."

CHAPTER XIX.

OUR MARCH OVER LAND AND SEA.

We had our boats to prepare now for a long and adventurous navigation. They were so small and heavily laden as hardly to justify much confidence in their buoyancy; but, besides this, they were split with frost and warped by sunshine, and fairly open at the seams. They were to be calked, and swelled, and launched, and stowed, before we could venture to embark in them. A rainy south-wester, too, which had met us on our arrival, was now spreading with its black nimbus over the bay, and it looked as if we were to be storm-stayed on the precarious ice beach. It was a time of anxiety, but to me personally of comparative rest. I resumed my journal:—

"*July* 18.—The Esquimaux are camped by our side,—the whole settlement of Etah congregated around the 'big caldron' of Cape Alexander, to bid us good-bye. There are Metek and Nualik his wife, our old acquaintance Mrs Eider-duck, and their five children, commencing with Myouk, my body-guard, and ending with the ventricose little Accomodah. There is Nessark and Anak his wife; and Tellerk the 'Right Arm,' and Amaunalik his wife; and Sip-su, and Marsumah and Aningnah—and who not? I can name them every one, and they know us as well. We have found brothers in a strange land.

"Each one has a knife, or a file, or a saw, or some such treasured keepsake; and the children have a lump of soap, the greatest of all great medicines. The merry little urchins break in upon me even now as I am writing—'Kuyanake, kuyanake, Nalegak-soak!' 'Thank you, thank you, big chief!' while Myouk is crowding fresh presents of raw birds on me as if I could eat for ever, and poor Aningnah is crying beside the tent-curtain, wiping her eyes on a bird skin!

"My heart warms to these poor, dirty, miserable, yet happy beings, so long our neighbours, and of late so staunchly our friends. Theirs is no affectation of regret. There are twenty-two of them around me, all busy in good offices to the Docto Kayens; and there are only two women and the old blind patriarch Kresuk, 'Drift-wood,' left behind at the settlement.

"But see! more of them are coming up—boys ten years old pushing forward babies on their sledges. The whole nation is gipsying with us upon the icy meadows.

"We cook for them in our big camp-kettle; they sleep

in the *Red Eric:* a berg close at hand supplies them with water; and thus, rich in all that they value,—sleep, and food, and drink, and companionship,—with their treasured short-lived summer sun above them, the *beau ideal* and sum of Esquimaux blessings, they seem supremely happy.

" Whatever may have been the faults of these Esquimaux heretofore, stealing was the only grave one. Treachery they may have conceived; and I have reason to believe that, under superstitious fears of an evil influence from our presence, they would at one time have been glad to destroy us. But the day of all this has passed away. When trouble came to us and to them, and we bent ourselves to their habits,—when we looked to them to procure us fresh meat, and they found at our poor Oomiak-soak shelter and protection during their wild bear-hunts,—then we were so blended in our interests as well as modes of life, that every trace of enmity wore away. God knows that since they professed friendship—albeit the imaginary powers of the angekok-soak and the marvellous six-shooter which attested them may have had their influence—never have friends been more true. Although, since Ohlsen's death, numberless articles of inestimable value to them have been scattered upon the ice unwatched, they have not stolen a nail. It was only yesterday that Metek, upon my alluding to the manner in which property of all sorts was exposed without pilfering, explained through Petersen, in these two short sentences, the argument of their morality:—

"' You have done us good. We are not hungry; we will not take (steal).——You have done us good; we want to help you; we are friends.'"

I made my last visit to Etah while we were waiting the issue of the storm. I saw old Kresuk (Drift-wood) the blind man, and listened to his long good bye talk. I had passed with the Esquimaux as an angekok, in virtue of some simple exploits of natural magic; and it was one of the regular old-times entertainments of our visitors at the brig, to see my hand terrible with blazing ether, while it lifted nails with the magnet. I tried now to communicate a portion of my wonder-working talent. I made a lens of ice before them, and "drew down the sun," so as to light the moss under their kolupsut. I did not quite understand old Kresuk, and I was not quite sure he understood himself. But I trusted to the others to explain to him what I had done, and burned the back of his hand for a testimony in the most friendly manner. After all which, with a reputation for wisdom which I dare say will live in their short annals, I wended my way to the brig again.

We renewed our queries about Hans, but could get no further news of him. The last story is, that the poor boy and his better-half were seen leaving Petcravik, "the halting-place," in company with Shang-hu and one of his big sons. Lover as he was, and nalegak by the all-hail hereafter, joy go with him, for he was a right good fellow.

We had quite a scene distributing our last presents. My amputating knives, the great gift of all, went to Metek and Nessark; but every one had something as his special prize. Our dogs went to the community at large, as tenants in common, except Toodlamik and Whitey, our representative dogs through very many trials; I could not part with them, the leaders of my team.

And now it only remained for us to make our farewell to these desolate and confiding people. I gathered them round me on the ice-beach, and talked to them as brothers for whose kindness I had still a return to make. I told them what I knew of the tribes from which they were separated by the glacier and the sea, of the resources that abounded in those less ungenial regions not very far off to the south, the greater duration of daylight, the less intensity of the cold, the facilities of the hunt, the frequent drift-wood, the kayack, and the fishing-net. I tried to explain to them how, under bold and cautious guidance, they might reach there in a few seasons of patient march. I gave them drawings of the coast, with its headlands and hunting-grounds, as far as Cape Shackleton, and its best camping-stations from Red Head to the Danish settlements.

They listened with breathless interest, closing their circle round me; and, as Petersen described the big ussuk, the white whale, the bear, and the long open water hunts with the kayack and the rifle, they looked at each other with a significance not to be misunderstood. They would anxiously have had me promise that I would some day return and carry a load of them down to the settlements; and I shall not wonder if—guided perhaps by Hans—they hereafter attempt the journey without other aid.

It was in the soft subdued light of a Sunday evening, June 17, that, after hauling our boats with much hard labour through the hummocks, we stood beside the open sea-way. Before midnight we had launched the *Red Eric*, and given three cheers for Henry Grinnell and "homeward bound," unfurling all our flags.

But we were not yet to embark; for the gale which had been long brooding now began to dash a heavy *wind-lipper* against the floe, and obliged us to retreat before it, hauling our boats back with each fresh breakage of the ice. It rose more fiercely, and we were obliged to give way before it still more. Our goods, which had been stacked upon the ice, had to be carried further inward. We worked our way back thus, step by step, before the breaking ice, for about two hundred yards. At last it became apparent that the men must sleep and rest, or sink; and, giving up for the present all thoughts of embarking, I hauled the boats at once nearly a mile from the water's edge, where a large iceberg was frozen tight in the floes.

But here we were still pursued. All the next night it blew fearfully, and at last our berg crashed away through the broken ice, and our asylum was destroyed. Again we fell to hauling back the boats; until, fearing that the continuance of the gale might induce a ground-swell, which would have been fatal to us, I came to a halt near the slope of a low iceberg, on which I felt confident that we could haul up, in case of the entire disruption of the floes. The entire area was already intersected with long cracks, and the surface began to show a perceptible undulation beneath our feet.

It was well for us I had not gratified the men by taking the outside track; we should certainly have been rafted off into the storm, and without an apparent possibility of escape.

I climbed to the summit of the berg; but it was impossible to penetrate the obscurity of mist, and spray, and cloud further than a thousand yards. The sea tore the ice up almost to the very base of the berg, and all around it looked like one vast tumultuous caldron, the ice-tables crashing together in every possible position with deafening clamour.

The gale died away to a calm, and the water became as tranquil as if the gale had never been. All hands were called to prepare for embarking. The boats were stowed, and the cargo divided between them equally; the sledges unlashed and slung outside the gunwales; and on Tuesday the 19th, at 4 P.M., with the bay as smooth as a garden-lake, I put off in the *Faith*. She was followed by the *Red*

Eric on our quarter, and the *Hope* astern. In the *Faith* I had with me Mr M'Gary, and Petersen, Hickey, Stephenson, and Whipple. Mr Brooks was in the *Hope*, with Hayes, Sontag, Morton, Goodfellow, and Blake. Bonsall, Riley, and Godfrey made the crew of the *Eric*.

The wind freshened as we doubled the westernmost point of Cape Alexander, and, as we looked out on the expanse of the sound, we saw the kitty-wakes and the ivory-gulls and jagers dipping their wings in the curling waves. They seemed the very same birds we had left two years before screaming and catching fish in the beautiful water. We tried to make our first rest at Sutherland Island; but we found it so barricaded by the precipitous ice-belt that it was impossible to land. I clambered myself from the boat's mast upon the platform and filled our kettles with snow, and then, after cooking our supper in the boats, we stood away for Hakluyt. It was an ugly crossing: we had a short chopping sea from the south-east; and, after a while, the *Red Eric* swamped. Riley and Godfrey managed to struggle to the *Faith*, and Bonsall to the *Hope*: but it was impossible to remove the cargo of our little comrade; it was as much as we could do to keep her afloat and let her tow behind us. Just at this time, too, the *Hope* made a signal of distress; and Brooks hailed us to say that she was making water faster than he could free her.

The wind was hauling round to the westward, and we could not take the sea abeam. But, as I made a rapid survey of the area around me, studded already with floating shreds of floe-ice, I saw ahead the low, grey blink of the pack. I remembered well the experience of our Beechy Island trip, and knew that the margin of these large fields is almost always broken by inlets of open water, which gave much the same sort of protection as the creeks and rivers of an adverse coast. We were fortunate in finding one of these, and fastening ourselves to an old floe, alongside of which our weary men turned in to sleep without hauling up the boats.

When Petersen and myself returned from an unsuccessful hunt upon the ice, we found them still asleep, in spite of a cold and drizzling rain that might have stimulated wakefulness. I did not disturb them till eight o'clock. We then retreated from our breakwater of refuge, generally pulling along by the boat-hooks, but sometimes dragging our boats over the ice; and at last, bending to our oars as the water opened, reached the shore of Hakluyt Island.

In the morning of the 22d we pushed forward for Northumberland Island, and succeeded in reaching it a little to the eastward of my former landing-place.

We crossed Murchison Channel on the 23d, and encamped for the night on the land-floe at the base of Cape Parry; a hard day's travel, partly by tracking over ice, partly through tortuous and zigzag leads. The next day gave us admirable progress. The ice opened in leads before us, somewhat tortuous, but, on the whole, favouring, and for sixteen hours I never left the helm. We were all of us exhausted when the day's work came to a close.

The next day's progress was of course slow and wearisome, pushing through alternate ice and water for the land-belt. We fastened at last to the great floe near the shore, making our harbour in a crack which opened with the changes of tide.

The imperfect diet of the party was showing itself more and more in the decline of their muscular power. They seemed scarcely aware of it themselves, and referred the difficulty they found in dragging and pushing to something uncommon about the ice or sludge, rather than to their own weakness. But, as we endeavoured to renew our labours through the morning fog, belted in on all sides by ice-fields so distorted and rugged as to defy our efforts to cross them, the truth seemed to burst upon every one. We had lost the feeling of hunger, and were almost satisfied with our pasty broth and the large draughts of tea which accompanied it. I was anxious to send our small boat, the *Eric*, across to the lumme-hill of Appah, where I knew from the Esquimaux we should find plenty of birds; but the strength of the party was insufficient to drag her.

We were sorely disheartened, and could only wait for the fog to rise, in the hope of some smoother platform than that which was about us, or some lead that might save us the painful labour of tracking. I had climbed an iceberg, and there was nothing in view except Dalrymple Rock, with its red brassy face towering in the unknown distance. But I hardly got back to my boat, before a gale struck us from the north-west, and a floe, taking upon a tongue of ice about a mile to the north of us, began to swing upon it like a pivot, and close slowly in upon our narrow resting-place.

At first our own floe also was driven before the wind; but in a little while it encountered the stationary ice at the foot of the very rock itself. On the instant the wildest imaginable ruin rose around us. The men sprang mechanically each one to his station, bearing back the boats and stores; but I gave up for the moment all hope of our escape. It was not a nip, such as is familiar to Arctic navigators; but the whole platform where we stood, and for hundreds of yards on every side of us, crumbled, and crushed, and piled, and tossed itself madly under the pressure. I do not believe that of our little body of men, all of them disciplined in trials, able to measure danger while combating it,—I do not believe there is one who this day can explain how or why—hardly when, in fact—we found ourselves afloat. We only know that in the midst of a clamour utterly indescribable, through which the braying of a thousand trumpets could no more have been heard than the voice of a man, we were shaken, and raised, and whirled, and let down again in a swelling waste of broken hummocks, and, as the men grasped their boat-hooks in the stillness that followed, the boats eddied away in a tumultuous skreed of ice, and snow, and water.

We were borne along in this manner as long as the unbroken remnant of the in-shore floe continued revolving,—utterly powerless, and catching a glimpse every now and then of the brazen headland that looked down on us through the snowy sky. At last the floe brought up against the rocks, the looser fragments that hung round it began to separate, and we were able by oars and boat-hooks to force our battered little flotilla clear of them. To our joyful surprise, we soon found ourselves in a stretch of the land-water wide enough to give us rowing-room, and with the assured promise of land close ahead.

At three o'clock the tide was high enough for us to scale the ice-cliff. One by one we pulled up the boats upon a narrow shelf, the whole sixteen of us uniting at each pull. We were too much worn down to unload; but a deep and narrow gorge opened in the cliffs almost at the spot where we clambered up; and, as we pushed the boats into it on an even keel, the rocks seemed to close above our heads, until an abrupt turn in the course of the ravine placed a protecting cliff between us and the gale. We were completely encaved.

Just as we had brought in the last boat, the *Red Eric*, and were shoring her up with blocks of ice, a long-unused, but familiar and unmistakable sound startled and gladdened every ear, and a flock of eiders darkening the sky for a moment passed swiftly in front of us. We knew that we must be at their breeding-grounds; and as we turned in wet and hungry to our long-coveted sleep, it was only to dream of eggs and abundance.

We remained almost three days in our crystal retreat, gathering eggs at the rate of twelve hundred a day. Outside, the storm raged without intermission, and our egg-hunters found it difficult to keep their feet; but a merrier set of gourmands than were gathered within never surfeited on genial diet.

On the 3d of July the wind began to moderate, though the snow still fell heavily; and the next morning, after a patriotic egg-nog, the liquor borrowed grudgingly from our alcohol-flask, and diluted till it was worthy of temperance praise, we lowered our boats, and bade a grateful farewell to "Weary Man's Rest." We rowed to the south-east end of Wostenholme Island; but the tide left us there, and we moved to the ice-foot.

In the meantime, the birds, which had been so abundant when we left Dalrymple's Island, and which we had counted on for a continuous store, seemed to have been driven off by the storm. We were again reduced to short daily rations of bread-dust, and I was aware that the change of diet could not fail to tell upon the strength and energies of the party. I determined to keep in-shore, in spite of the barricades of ice, in the hope of renewing, to some extent at least, our supplies of game. We were fifty-two hours in forcing this rugged passage: a most painful labour, which, but for the disciplined endurance of the men, might well have been deemed impracticable.

Once through the barrier, the leads began to open again,

and on the 11th we found ourselves approaching Cape Dudley Digges, with a light breeze from the north-west. It looked for some hours as if our troubles were over, when a glacier came in sight not laid down on the charts, whose tongue of floe extended still further out to sea than the one we had just passed with so much labour. Our first resolve was to double it at all hazards, for our crews were too much weakened to justify another tracking through the hummocks, and the soft snow which covered the land-floes was an obstacle quite insuperable. Nevertheless, we forced our way into a lead of sludge, mingled with the comminuted ice of the glacier; but the only result was a lesson of gratitude for our escape from it. Our frail and weather-worn boats were quite unequal to the duty.

I again climbed the nearest berg,—for these ice-mountains were to us like the look-out hills of men at home,—and surveyed the ice to the south far on toward Cape York. My eyes never looked on a spectacle more painful. We were in advance of the season: the floes had not broken up. There was no "western water." Here, in a *cul-de-sac*, between two barriers, both impassable to men in our condition, with stores miserably inadequate and strength broken down, we were to wait till the tardy summer should open to us a way.

I headed for the cliffs. Desolate and frowning as they were, it was better to reach them and halt upon the inhospitable shore than await the fruitless ventures of the sea. A narrow lead, a mere fissure at the edge of the land-ice, ended opposite a low platform; we had traced its whole extent, and it landed us close under the shadow of the precipitous shore.

Providence Retreat, as I called this spot, abounded in life. We found the lumme, nearly as large as canvasbacks, and, as we thought, altogether sweeter and more juicy; their eggs, well known as delicacies on the Labrador coast; the cochlearia, growing superbly on the guano-coated surface;—all of them in endless abundance: imagine such a combination of charms for scurvy-broken, hungry-stricken men.

I could not allow the fuel for a fire, our slush and tallow being reduced to very little more than a hundred pounds. The more curious in the art of cooking made experiments upon the organic matters within their reach,—the dried nests of the kitty-wake, the sods of poa, the heavy mosses, and the fatty skins of the birds around us. But they would none of them burn; and the most fastidious consoled himself at last with the doubt whether heat, though concentrating flavour, might not impair some other excellence. We limited ourselves to an average of a bird a-piece per meal,—of choice, not of necessity,—and renewed the zest of the table with the best salad in the world—raw eggs and cochlearia.

It was one glorious holiday, our week at Providence Halt; so full of refreshment and all-happy thoughts, that I never allowed myself to detract from it by acknowledging that it was other than premeditated. There were only two of the party who had looked out with me on the bleak ice-field ahead, and them I had pledged to silence.

On the 18th of July the aspects of the ice about us gave me the hope of progress. We had prepared ourselves for the new encounter with the sea and its trials by laying in a store of lumme; two hundred and fifty of which had been duly skinned, spread open, and dried on the rocks, as the *entremets* of our bread-dust and tallow.

My journal tells of disaster in its record of our setting-out. In launching the *Hope* from the frail and perishing ice-wharf on which we found our first refuge from the gale, she was precipitated into the sludge below, carrying away rail and bulwark, losing overboard our best shot-gun, Bonsall's favourite, and, worst of all, that universal favourite, our kettle,—soup-kettle, paste-kettle, tea-kettle, water-kettle, in one. I may mention, before I pass, that the kettle found its substitute and successor in the remains of a tin-can which a good aunt of mine had filled with ginger-nuts two years before, and which had long survived the condiments that once gave it dignity. "Such are the uses of adversity."

Our descent to the coast followed the margin of the fast ice. After passing the Crimson Cliffs of Sir John Ross, it wore almost the dress of a holiday excursion,—a rude one perhaps, yet truly one in feeling. Our course, except where a protruding glacier interfered with it, was nearly parallel to the shore. The birds along it were rejoicing in the young summer, and when we halted it was upon some green-clothed cape near a stream of water from the ice-fields above. Our sportsmen would clamber up the cliffs and come back laden with little auks; great generous fires of turf, that cost nothing but the toil of gathering, blazed merrily; and our happy oarsmen, after a long day's work, made easy by the promise ahead, would stretch themselves in the sunshine and dream happily away till called to the morning wash and prayers. We enjoyed it the more, for we all of us knew that it could not last.

We reached Cape York on the 21st, after a tortuous but romantic travel through a misty atmosphere. Here the land-leads ceased, with the exception of some small and scarcely-practicable openings near the shore, which were evidently owing to the wind that prevailed for the time.

Everything bore proof of the late development of the season. The red snow was a fortnight behind its time. A fast floe extended with numerous tongues far out to the south and east. The only question was between a new rest for the shore-ices to open, or a desertion of the coast, and a trial of the open water to the west.

We sent off a detachment to see whether the Esquimaux might not be passing the summer at Episok, behind the glacier of Cape Imalik, and began an inventory of our stock on hand.

On their return they gave us no reason to hesitate. The Esquimaux had not been there for several years. There were no birds in the neighbourhood.

I called my officers together, explained to them the motives which governed me, and prepared to re-embark. The boats were hauled up, examined carefully, and, as far as our means permitted, repaired. The *Red Eric* was stripped of her outfit and cargo, to be broken up for fuel when the occasion should come. A large beacon-cairn was built on an eminence, open to view from the south and west; and a red flannel shirt, spared with some reluctance, was hoisted as a pennant to draw attention to the spot. Here I deposited a succinct record of our condition and purposes, and then directed our course south by west into the ice-fields.

I was awakened one evening from a weary sleep in my fox-skins, to discover that we had fairly lost our way. The officer at the helm of the leading boat, misled by the irregular shape of a large iceberg that crossed his track, had lost the main lead some time before, and was steering shoreward far out of the true course. The little canal in which he had locked us was hardly two boats'-lengths across, and lost itself not far off in a feeble zigzag both behind and before us: it was evidently closing, and we could not retreat.

Without apprising the men of our misadventure, I ordered the boats to be hauled up, and, under pretence of drying the clothing and stores, made a camp on the ice. A few hours after, the weather cleared enough for the first time to allow a view of the distance, and M'Gary and myself climbed a berg some three hundred feet high for the purpose. It was truly fearful: we were deep in the recesses of the bay, surrounded on all sides by stupendous icebergs and tangled floe-pieces. My sturdy second officer, not naturally impressible, and long accustomed to the vicissitudes of whaling life, shed tears at the prospect.

There was but one thing to be done: cost what it might, we must harness our sledges again and retrace our way to the westward. One sledge had been already used for firewood; the *Red Eric*, to which it had belonged, was now cut up, and her light cedar planking laid upon the floor of the other boats; and we went to work with the rue-raddies as in the olden time. It was not till the third toilsome day was well spent that we reached the berg which had bewildered our helmsman. We hauled over its tongue, and joyously embarked again upon a free lead, with a fine breeze from the north.

Our little squadron was now reduced to two boats. The land to the northward was no longer visible; and whenever I left the margin of the "fast" to avoid its deep sinuosities, I was obliged to trust entirely to the compass. We had at least eight days' allowance of fuel on board; but our provisions were running very low, and we met few birds, and failed to secure any larger game. We saw several large seals upon the ice, but they were too watchful for us; and on two occasions we came upon the walrus sleeping,—once within actual lance-thrust; but the animal charged in the teeth of his assailant and made good his retreat.

Although the low diet and exposure to wet had again reduced our party, there was no apparent relaxation of energy; and it was not until some days later that I found their strength seriously giving way.

I well remember our look of blank amazement as, one day, the order being given to haul the *Hope* over a tongue of ice, we found that she would not budge. At first I thought it was owing to the wetness of the snow-covered surface in which her runners were; but, as there was a heavy gale blowing outside, and I was extremely anxious to get her on to a larger floe to prevent being drifted off, I lightened her cargo and set both crews upon her. In the land of promise off Crimson Cliffs, such a force would have trundled her like a wheelbarrow: we could almost have borne her upon our backs. Now, with incessant labour and standing hauls, she moved at a snail's pace.

The *Faith* was left behind, and barely escaped destruction. The outside pressure cleft the floe asunder, and we saw our best boat, with all our stores, drifting rapidly away from us. The sight produced an almost hysterical impression upon our party. Two days' want of bread, I am sure, would have destroyed us; and we had now left us but eight pounds of shot in all. To launch the *Hope* again, and rescue her comrade or share her fortunes, would have been the instinct of other circumstances; but it was out of the question now. Happily, before we had time to ponder our loss, a flat cake of ice eddied round near the floe we were upon; M'Gary and myself sprang to it at the moment, and succeeded in floating it across the chasm in time to secure her. The rest of the crew rejoined her by only scrambling over the crushed ice as we brought her in at the hummock-lines.

CHAPTER XX.

STARVATION—PLENTY—THE ESCAPE WELCOME.

Things grew worse and worse with us: the old difficulty of breathing came back again, and our feet swelled to such an extent that we were obliged to cut open our canvas boots. But the symptom which gave me most uneasiness was our inability to sleep. A form of low fever which hung by us when at work had been kept down by the thoroughness of our daily rest; all my hopes of escape were in the refreshing influences of the halt.

It was at this crisis of our fortunes that we saw a large seal floating—as is the custom of these animals—on a small patch of ice, and seemingly asleep. It was an ussuk, and so large that I at first mistook it for a walrus. Signal was made for the *Hope* to follow astern, and, trembling with anxiety, we prepared to crawl down upon him.

Petersen, with the large English rifle, was stationed in the bow, and stockings were drawn over the oars as mufflers. As we neared the animal, our excitement became so intense that the men could hardly keep stroke. I had a set of signals for such occasions, which spared us the noise of the voice; and when about three hundred yards off, the oars were taken in, and we moved on in deep silence with a single scull astern.

He was not asleep, for he reared his head when we were almost within rifle-shot; and to this day I can remember the hard, care-worn, almost despairing expression of the men's thin faces as they saw him move: their lives de-depended on his capture.

I depressed my hand nervously, as a signal for Petersen to fire. M'Gary hung upon his oar, and the boat, slowly but noiselessly sagging ahead, seemed to me without certain range. Looking at Petersen, I saw that the poor fellow was paralysed by his anxiety, trying vainly to obtain a rest for his gun against the cut-water of the boat. The seal rose on his four-flippers, gazed at us for a moment with frightened curiosity, and coiled himself for a plunge. At that instant, simultaneously with the crack of our rifle, he relaxed his long length on the ice, and, at the very brink of the water, his head fell helpless to one side.

I would have ordered another shot, but no discipline could have controlled the men. With a wild yell, each vociferating according to his own impulse, they urged both boats upon the floes. A crowd of hands seized the seal and bore him up to safer ice. The men seemed half crazy; I had not realised how much we were reduced by absolute famine. They ran over the floe, crying and laughing, and brandishing their knives. It was not five minutes before every man was sucking his bloody fingers or eating long strips of raw blubber.

That night, on the large halting-floe, to which, in contempt of the dangers of drifting, we happy men had hauled our boats, two entire planks of the *Red Eric* were devoted to a grand cooking-fire, and we enjoyed a rare and savage feast.

This was our last experience of the disagreeable effects of hunger. In the words of George Stephenson, " the charm was broken, and the dogs were safe." The dogs I have said little about, for none of us liked to think of them. The poor creatures, Toodla and Whitey, had been taken with us as last resources against starvation. They were, as M'Gary worded it, "meat on the hoof," and "able to carry their own fat over the floes." Once, near Weary Man's Rest, I had been on the point of killing them; but they had been the leaders of our winter's team, and we could not bear the sacrifice.

I need not detail our journey any further. Within a day or two we shot another seal, and from that time forward had a full supply of food.

And now, with the apparent certainty of reaching our homes, came that nervous apprehension which follows upon hope long deferred. I could not trust myself to take the outside passage, but timidly sought the quiet-water channels running deep into the archipelago which forms a sort of labyrinth along the coast.

Thus it was that at one of our sleeping-halts upon the rocks—for we still adhered to the old routine—Petersen awoke me with a story. He had just seen and recognised a native, who, in his frail kayack, was evidently seeking eider-down among the islands. The man had once been an inmate of his family. "Paul Zacharias, don't you know me? I'm Carl Petersen!" "No," said the man; "his wife says he's dead;" and, with a stolid expression of wonder, he stared for a moment at the long beard that loomed at him through the fog, and paddled away with all the energy of fright.

Two days after this, a mist had settled down upon the islands which embayed us, and when it lifted we found ourselves rowing, in lazy time, under the shadow of Karkamoot. Just then a familiar sound came to us over the water. We had often listened to the screeching of the gulls or the bark of the fox, and mistaken it for the "Huk" of the Esquimaux; but this had about it an inflection not to be mistaken, for it died away in the familiar cadence of a "halloo."

"Listen, Petersen! oars, men!" "What is it?"—and he listened quietly at first, and then, trembling, said, in a half whisper, "Dannemarkers!"

By-and-by—for we must have been pulling a good half-hour—the single mast of a small shallop showed itself; and Petersen, who had been very quiet and grave, burst out into an incoherent fit of crying, only relieved by broken exclamations of mingled Danish and English. "'Tis the Upernavik oil-boat! The Fraulein Flaischer! Carlie Mossyn, the cooper, must be on his road to Kingatok for blubber."

It was Carlie Mossyn, sure enough. The quiet routine of a Danish settlement is the same, year after year, and Petersen had hit upon the exact state of things. The *Mariane* was at Proven, and Carlie Mossyn had come up in the Fraulein Flaischer to get the year's supply of blubber from Kingatok.

Here we first got our cloudy, vague idea of what had passed in the big world during our absence. The friction of its fierce rotation had not much disturbed this little outpost of civilisation, and we thought it a sort of blunder as he told us that France and England were leagued with the Mussulman against the Greek Church. He was a good Lutheran, this assistant cooper, and all news with him had a theological complexion.

"What of America, eh, Petersen?"—and we all looked, waiting for him to interpret the answer.

"America?" said Carlie; "we don't know much of tha.

country here, for they have no whalers on the coast; but a steamer and a barque passed up a fortnight ago, and have gone out into the ice to seek your party."

How gently all the lore of this man oozed out of him! he seemed an oracle, as, with hot-tingling fingers pressed against the gunwale of the boat, we listened to his words. "Sebastopol is not taken." Where and what was Sebastopol?

But "Sir John Franklin?" There we were at home again,—our own delusive little speciality rose uppermost. Franklin's party, or traces of the dead which represented it, had been found nearly a thousand miles to the south **of** where we had been searching for them. He knew it; for the priest had a German newspaper which told all about it. And so we "out oars" again, and rowed into the fogs.

Another sleeping-halt has passed, and we have all washed clean at the fresh-water basins, and furbished up our ragged furs and woollens. Kasarsoak, the snow top of Sanderson's Hope, shows itself above the mists, and we hear the yelling of the dogs. Petersen had been foreman of the settlement, and he calls my attention, with a sort of pride, to the tolling of the workmen's bell. It is six o'clock. We are nearing the end of our trials. Can it be a dream?

We hugged the land by the big harbour, turned the corner by the old brew-house, and, in the midst of a crowd of children, hauled our boats for the last time upon the rocks.

For eighty-four days we had lived in the open air. Our habits were hard and weather-worn. We could not remain within the four walls of a house without a distressing sense of suffocation. But we drank coffee that night before many a hospitable threshold, and listened again and again to the hymn of welcome, which, sung by many voices, greeted our deliverance.

CHAPTER XXI.

CONCLUSION.

We received all manner of kindness from the Danes of Upernavik. They gave us many details of the expeditions in search of Sir John Franklin, and added the painful news that my gallant friend and comrade, Bellot, had perished in a second crusade to save him. We knew each other by many common sympathies: I had divided with him the hazards of mutual rescue among the ice-fields; and his last letter to me, just before I left New York, promised me the hope that we were to meet again in Baffin's Bay, and that he would unite himself with our party as a volunteer. The French service never lost a more chivalrous spirit.

The Danish vessel was not ready for her homeward journey till the 4th of September; but the interval was well spent in regaining health and gradually accustoming ourselves to in-door life and habits. It is a fact, which the physiologist will not find it difficult to reconcile with established theories, that we were all more prostrated by the repose and comfort of our new condition than we had been by nearly three months of constant exposure and effort.

On the 6th I left Upernavik, with all our party, in the *Mariane*, a staunch but antiquated little barque, under the command of Captain Ammondson, who promised to drop us at the Shetland Islands. Our little boat, the *Faith*, which was regarded by all of us as a precious relic, took passage along with us. Except the furs on our backs, and the documents that recorded our labours and our trials, it was all we brought back of the *Advance* and her fortunes.

On the 11th we arrived at Godhavn, and had a characteristic welcome from my excellent friend, Mr Olrik. The *Mariane* had stopped only to discharge a few stores and receive her papers of clearance; but her departure was held back to the latest moment, in hopes of receiving news of Captain Hartstene's squadron, which had not been heard of since the 21st of July.

We were upon the eve of setting out, however, when the look-out man at the hill-top announced a steamer in the distance. It drew near, with a barque in tow, and we soon recognised the stars and stripes of our own country. The *Faith* was lowered for the last time into the water, and the little flag which had floated so near the poles of both hemispheres, opened once more to the breeze. With Brooks at the tiller, and Mr Olrik at my side, followed by all the boats of the settlement, we went out to meet them.

Never did the men lay to their oars more heartily. We neared the squadron and the gallant men that had come out to seek us; we could see the scars which their own ice-battles had impressed on the vessels; we knew the gold lace of the officers' cap-bands, and discerned the groups who, glass in hand, were evidently regarding us.

Presently we were alongside. An officer, whom I shall ever remember as a cherished friend, Captain Hartstene, hailed a little man in a ragged flannel shirt, "Is that Dr Kane?" and with the "Yes!" that followed, the rigging was manned by our countrymen, and cheers welcomed us back to the social world of love which they represented.

William P. Nimmo & Co., Edinburgh.

NIMMO'S HALF-CROWN REWARD BOOKS.

Extra foolscap 8vo, cloth elegant, gilt edges, Illustrated, price 2s. 6d. each.

1. Memorable Wars of Scotland. By Patrick Fraser Tytler, F.R.S.E., Author of 'The History of Scotland,' etc.
2. Seeing the World: A Young Sailor's own Story. By CHARLES NORDHOFF, Author of 'The Young Man-of-War's-Man.'
3. The Martyr Missionary: Five Years in China. By Rev. CHARLES P. BUSH, M.A.
4. My New Home: A Woman's Diary.
5. Home Heroines: Tales for Girls. By T. S. Arthur, Author of 'Life's Crosses,' etc.
6. Lessons from Women's Lives. By Sarah J. Hale.
7. The Roseville Family. A Historical Tale of the Eighteenth Century. By Mrs. A. S. ORR, Author of 'Mountain Patriots,' etc.
8. Leah. A Tale of Ancient Palestine. Illustrative of the Story of Naaman the Syrian. By Mrs. A. S. ORR.
9. Champions of the Reformation: The Stories of their Lives. By JANET GORDON.
10. The History of Two Wanderers; or, Cast Adrift.
11. The Vicar of Wakefield. By Oliver Goldsmith.
12. The Miner's Son, and Margaret Vernon. By M. M. POLLARD, Author of 'The Minister's Daughter,' etc. etc.
13. How Frank began to Climb the Ladder. By Charles BRUCE, Author of 'Lame Felix,' etc.
14. The Golden Country; or, Conrad and the Princess. A Tale for the Young. By JAMES MASON.
15. Aunt Ann's Stories. Edited by L. Loughborough.
16. The Snow-Sweepers' Party, and the Tale of Old Tubbins. By R. ST. JOHN CORBET, Author of 'Minco Pie Island.'
17. The Story of Elise Marcel. A Tale for Girls.
18. A Child's Corner Book: Stories for Boys and Girls. By RICHARD ROWE, Author of 'Episodes in an Obscure Life,' 'Jack Afloat and Ashore,' etc.
19. The Lucky Bag: Stories for the Young. By Richard ROWE, Author of 'The Tower on the Tor,' etc.

Complete Catalogues of W. P. NIMMO & CO.'S Publications may be had post free on application.

William P. Nimmo & Co., Edinburgh.

NIMMO'S
HOME AND SCHOOL REWARD BOOKS.

Foolscap 8vo, Illustrated, elegantly bound in cloth extra, bevelled boards, gilt back and side, gilt edges, price 2s. each.

1. **Guiding Lights: Lives of the Great and Good.** By F. E. Cooke, Author of 'Footprints.'
2. **Heroes of Charity: Records from the Lives of** Merciful Men whose Righteousness has not been Forgotten. By JAMES F. COBB, F.R.G.S., Author of 'Stories of Success,' etc.
3. **Afloat and Ashore with Sir Walter Raleigh.** By Mrs. HARDY (JANET GORDON), Author of 'Champions of the Reformation,' etc.
4. **Philip Walton; or, Light at Last.** By the Author of 'Meta Franz,' etc.
5. **The Standard-Bearer. A Tale of the Times of** Constantine the Great. By ELLEN PALMER.
6. **Mountain Patriots. A Tale of the Reformation** in Savoy. By Mrs. A. S. ORR.
7. **Picture Lessons by the Divine Teacher; or, Illus-** trations of the Parables of our Lord. By PETER GRANT, D.D.
8. **Taken up: A Tale for Boys and Girls.** By Alfred WHYMPER.
9. **Stories told in a Fisherman's Cottage.** By Ellen PALMER, Author of 'The Standard-Bearer,' etc. etc.
10. **Diversions of Hollycot; or, The Mother's Art of** Thinking. By Mrs. JOHNSTONE, Author of 'Nights of the Round Table,' 'Clan Albin,' etc.
11. **The King's Highway; or, Illustrations of the** Commandments. By the Rev. RICHARD NEWTON, D.D., Author of 'The Best Things,' etc.
12. **Nature's Wonders.** By the Rev. Richard Newton, D.D., Author of 'The King's Highway,' etc.

William P. Nimmo & Co., Edinburgh.

NIMMO'S
ONE SHILLING ILLUSTRATED JUVENILE BOOKS.

Foolscap 8vo, Coloured Frontispieces, handsomely bound in cloth, Illuminated, price 1s. each.

1. Four Little People and their Friends.
2. Elizabeth; or, The Exiles of Siberia. A Tale from the French of Madame Cottin.
3. Paul and Virginia. From the French of Bernardin Saint-Pierre.
4. Little Threads: Tangle Thread, Golden Thread, and Silver Thread.
5. Benjamin Franklin, the Printer Boy.
6. Barton Todd, and the Young Lawyer.
7. The Perils of Greatness: The Story of Alexander Menzikoff.
8. Little Crowns and How to Win Them. By Rev. Joseph A. Collier.
9. Great Riches: Nelly Rivers' Story. By Aunt Fanny.
10. The Right Way, and the Contrast.
11. The Daisy's First Winter. And other Stories. By H. Beecher Stowe.
12. The Man of the Mountain. And other Stories.
13. Better than Rubies. With 62 Illustrations.
14. Experience Teaches. And other Stories. With 39 Illustrations.
15. The Happy Recovery. And other Stories. With 26 Illustrations.
16. Gratitude and Probity. And other Stories. With 21 Illustrations.
17. The Two Brothers. And other Stories. With 13 Illustrations.
18. The Young Orator. And other Stories. With 9 Illustrations.
19. Simple Stories to Amuse and Instruct. With Illustrations.
20. The Three Friends. And other Stories. With Illustrations.
21. Sybil's Sacrifice. And other Stories. With 12 Illustrations.
22. The Old Shepherd. And other Stories for the Young. With Illustrations.
23. The Young Officer. And other Stories for the Young. With Illustrations.
24. The False Heir. And other Stories for the Young. With Illustrations.
25. The Old Farmhouse; or, Alice Morton's Home. And other Stories. By M. M. Pollard.
26. Twyford Hall; or, Rosa's Christmas Dinner, and what she did with it. By Charles Bruce.
27. The Discontented Weathercock. And other Stories for Children. By M. Jones.
28. Out at Sea. And other Stories. By Two Authors.
29. The Story of Waterloo; or, The Fall of Napoleon.
30. Sister Jane's Little Stories. Edited by Louisa Loughborough.
31. Uncle John's First Shipwreck; or, The Loss of the Brig 'Nellie.' By Charles Bruce, Author of 'Noble Mottoes,' 'The Book of Noble Englishwomen,' etc.
32. The History of a Lifeboat. By Richard Rowe, Author of 'The Tower on the Tor,' etc.

William P. Nimmo & Co., Edinburgh.

NIMMO'S
NINEPENNY SERIES FOR BOYS AND GIRLS.

In demy 18mo, with Illustrations, elegantly bound in cloth, price 9d. each.

This Series of Books will be found unequalled for genuine interest and value, and it is believed they will be eagerly welcomed by thoughtful children of both sexes. Parents may rest assured that each Volume teaches some noble lesson, or enforces some valuable truth.

1. In the Brave Days of Old; or, The Story of the Spanish Armada. For Boys and Girls.
2. The Lost Ruby. By the Author of 'The Basket of Flowers,' etc.
3. Leslie Ross; or, Fond of a Lark. By Charles Bruce.
4. My First and Last Voyage. By Benjamin Clarke.
5. Little Katie: A Fairy Story. By Charles Bruce.
6. Being Afraid. And other Stories for the Young. By Charles Stuart.
7. The Toll-Keepers. And other Stories for the Young. By Benjamin Clarke.
8. Dick Barford: A Boy who would go down Hill. By Charles Bruce.
9. Joan of Arc; or, The Story of a Noble Life. Written for Girls.
10. Helen Siddal: A Story for Children. By Ellen Palmer.
11. Mat and Sofie: A Story for Boys and Girls.
12. Peace and War. By the Author of 'The Basket of Flowers,' etc.
13. Perilous Adventures of a French Soldier in Algeria.
14. The Magic Glass; or, The Secret of Happiness.
15. Hawk's Dene: A Tale for Children. By Katharine E. May.
16. Little Maggie. And other Stories. By the Author of 'The Joy of Well-Doing,' etc. etc.
17. The Brother's Legacy; or, Better than Gold. By M. M. Pollard.
18. The Little Sisters; or, Jealousy. And other Stories for the Young. By the Author of 'Little Tales for Tiny Tots,' etc.
19. Kate's New Home. By Cecil Scott, Author of 'Chryssie Lyle,' etc.

⁎ The distinctive features are: The subjects of each Volume have been selected with a due regard to Instruction and Entertainment; they are well printed on fine paper; they are Illustrated with Coloured Frontispieces and beautiful Engravings; and they are elegantly bound.

www.ingramcontent.com/pod-product-compliance
Lightning Source LLC
Chambersburg PA
CBHW021814230426
43669CB00008B/748